The Magician's Glass
Ed Douglas

The Magician's Glass

Character and fate:
eight essays on climbing
and the mountain life

Ed Douglas

Vertebrate Publishing, Sheffield
www.v-publishing.co.uk

'There's something ever egotistical in mountaintops and towers, and all other grand and lofty things … which, like a magician's glass, to each and every man in turn but mirrors back his own mysterious self.'

Captain Ahab

The Magician's Glass

Ed Douglas

First published in 2017 by Vertebrate Publishing.

Vertebrate Publishing
Crescent House, 228 Psalter Lane, Sheffield S11 8UT.
www.v-publishing.co.uk

This book is a work of non-fiction based on the life, experiences and recollections of Ed Douglas.
In some limited cases the names of people, places, dates and sequences or the detail of events have been
changed solely to protect the privacy of others. The author has stated to the publishers that, except in
such minor respects not affecting the substantial accuracy of the work, the contents of the book are true.

A CIP catalogue record for this book is available from the British Library.

978-1-911342-48-9 (Print edition)
978-1-911342-49-6 (Ebook)

Design and production by Jane Beagley.
Vertebrate Publishing
www.v-publishing.co.uk

Vertebrate Publishing is committed to printing on paper from sustainable sources.

Printed and bound in the UK by T.J. International Ltd, Padstow, Cornwall.

Contents

Foreword

The Beguiling Mirror
Katie Ives

In April 2011, dark clouds dim the western sky above an unclimbed peak in the Changla Himal of Nepal. At nearly 6,000 metres, British alpinists Ed Douglas, Nick Colton and Julian Freeman-Attwood begin a long retreat down a tilted pane of ice and snow, through the melting drifts of a moraine gully. During the descent, Douglas observes the contrast between his own anxieties about the hazards and Colton's sheer delight in the wildness of the range. 'It was not that we were on a different mountain,' Douglas decides in 'The Magician's Glass', the first story in this collection; 'We were just seeing different things in the magician's mirror.'

The statement alludes to a famous scene in Herman Melville's novel *Moby Dick*, when Captain Ahab pauses before the gold doubloon he nailed to the mast of his ship – a prize for the first crew member who glimpses the elusive white whale, the object of their quest. Staring at images on the polished metal surface, Ahab wonders whether any transcendent significance lies behind the appearances of the world. 'There's something ever egotistical in mountaintops and towers, and all other grand and lofty things,' he muses, 'which, like a magician's glass, to each and every man in turn but mirrors back his own mysterious self.'

Like Ahab, climbers have long embarked on their adventures in search of meaning, as if the act of ascent could somehow reflect enigmatic truths about their place in the universe. And since the early days of alpine literature, mountains have lent themselves, as if inherently, to metaphors of giant mirrors: the way the sun glances off a cliff of faceted ice, a wall of burnished granite or a slope of glazed snow; how the light can cast a climber's silhouette against a shimmering cloud; how the myths of shifting cultures might appear projected over iconic summits.

Royal Robbins, in the foreword to a now-classic 1983 anthology, *Mirrors in the Cliffs*, explained, 'these stories hold the mirror up to nature, as the cliffs do a mirror to ourselves, enabling us to see inside, giving us the potential of a clearer view through to our spirit'. In that same volume, however, a 1937 story by John Menlove Edwards presented a more ambiguous vision, recounting a nightmare in which a climber sees himself split into two figures that spill their innards across the mountains. 'We will each make a little image from what we like to see of ourselves in the mirror of the hills,' he concluded, but all mirror images distort reality to some extent, and when the brilliant surfaces disintegrate, we may struggle to face what lies within.

Part of what has made Ed Douglas one of the world's best climbing journalists is his willingness to look closely at a multitude of human dreams and delusions, to try to understand what exists behind them and what their consequences might be. In many ways, this collection pieces together one trajectory of that quest. With unflinching persistence, Douglas examines the decades of fantasies that Western mountaineers brought with them to the Himalaya, reflections of their own cultural desires that have often obscured the real struggles of local expedition workers and communities. He describes the proliferation of media that turned some of the bold ascents of Tomaž Humar into a kind of surreal theatre until 'it seemed the image of himself he had created had started to consume him'. And as Douglas investigates the questions surrounding Ueli Steck's solitary climb on the south face of Annapurna, he considers the potential impact on the entire perception of mountaineering if someone 'at the core of the sport's image around the world' turned out to have fabricated an important story.

At the heart of many of these tales are the unknowns that emerge when illusions shatter and metaphors fade. As Douglas asks, 'If you look into the magician's glass and see yourself as you truly are, would you need it any longer?' Some alpinists, he concludes, might decide the risks are no longer worthwhile and abandon the mountains altogether, 'no longer [seeing] the sense in what they were doing'. They might come to believe that the beguiling mirror holds only an ultimate void of meaning. And yet the desire remains for something genuine that glimmers beyond all the shadowy reflections – evoked most hauntingly in Douglas's portrayal of Stefanie Egger, who, decades after her brother's death in Patagonia, still yearns for facts that vanished amid his climbing partner Cesare Maestri's disputed tales.

There's an indescribably numinous quality to the flow of Douglas's prose, a sense of radiance in the pauses between words, in the moments when a thought unfolds like a curled leaf, appearing suddenly translucent, golden. And there are hints throughout, of something like transcendence: the ray of light that turns Patrick Edlinger's body aglow right at the instant of a crux move; Kurt Albert's magician-like ability to transform the approaches to climbing again and again; Tomaž Humar's belief that mountaineering might offer a means to enlightenment, a 'third eye' that could allow him to intuit danger and glimpse some hidden spiritual reality.

As a writer, Douglas is often reticent about himself, preferring to focus on the experiences of others. It's in 'Lines of Beauty', the final story in this collection, that he comes the closest, perhaps, to expressing his own ideals. 'Imagination, creativity and thoughtfulness, the unquantifiable,' Douglas writes, 'these qualities ought to be part of mountaineering, or else the pursuit would be diminished. So should a feeling for the mountains, a sense of place, an attentiveness to the world outside your own story.' Of great artists such as Andy Parkin, Douglas adds, 'Some climbers, maybe only a few, are still searching for an understanding of our world that breaks through its shiny, commercial surface'. On the other side of those flickering images and self-reflecting walls, they might yet find possibilities of true wildness, mystery and transmutation, the ability to recast themselves – and perhaps the world – into new forms.

Parkin's reflected figure, seen in the rear-view mirror of a car, seems at first like that of an old man. And then, as Douglas watches him talk about a painting, Parkin appears all at once transfigured, his face flush with passion and youth, as if illuminated by a vision that flashes from some other realm. 'That's what I want to capture,' Douglas explains, 'the art of climbing, the spark of creativity, the shift in perspective that changes the way you – and others – view the world.'

The Magician's
Glass

2012

The heat is starting to build, and so I hurry on, placing my feet carefully in the crisp prints made by my companion. I can see him in the distance, outpacing me with clockwork efficiency, body stiffly upright, legs moving rapidly, like a toy automaton. Even though I step exactly where he has, at every fifth pace or so, the snow gives way, and I lurch forward, my leg buried up to the knee. I am heavier than he is, and my feet are only a little bigger, but still – it seems unfair.

Nick Colton and I are descending the trough of a lateral moraine banked out with snow. We woke late this morning at our advance base camp below an unclimbed mountain in western Nepal. After a long and unsuccessful summit bid we balanced aching limbs and a lazy breakfast with the need to descend before the snow softened.

Lost in the idea that we should have started earlier, I don't see Nick has stopped until I've almost caught him. He's on the crest of the moraine, reclining on a patch of tough grass, arms folded under his head, a broad grin on his face, his pale blue eyes shaded by a wide-brimmed hat. It will take us another half hour to reach base camp.

'We've timed this to perfection,' he says.

'Mmm,' I reply, resting on my ski sticks. I'm a little frustrated by our failure yesterday, and fretting about getting down before the snow melts. But Nick is simply happy to be in the moment, among a group of peaks no climber has seen before.

I crane my neck and spot Julian Attwood a short distance behind us. During an abseil yesterday, he and I had bickered about which rope to pull. We were both anxious about where we were and how to get away from it. Nick lay in the snow and mocked us with the kind of long, drawn-out exclamation reserved for petulant scraps in the playground. Jules and I laughed, but it made me think. It's not that we were on a different mountain, Nick and I. We were just seeing different things in the magician's mirror.

The day after our walk down to base camp, Nick and I are sprawled out in his cheap, borrowed Russian tent, which is already failing. The rest of his gear – apart from a brand-new pair of boots – is much older but self-evidently more durable. By his head is a tatty book of Sudoku puzzles. At any moment when his full attention isn't required, Nick will lie down and either start work on his current puzzle or go to sleep. He's now propped on an elbow lying on a worn, blue sleeping bag, the type I've seen displayed in a museum. 'I got it to go to Alaska,' he says.

'Remind me when that was?'

'1981.'

That was the year Nick made the first ascents of the west face of Huntington and the north face of the Rooster Comb, with Tim Leach. They were due to try a third difficult line on the Moonflower after that, but Nick's toes were battered from too much front-pointing. So they jogged up the west buttress of Denali instead, only to get stormbound in a snow cave. When Nick needed to defecate, his fellow snow-holers forced him out into the wind. He fell through the ceiling of a second snow cave, where he discovered a stockpile of long-abandoned food that kept them going through the bad weather.

That year was significant for another climb, this time unsuccessful, thousands of miles away at the head of one of the most inaccessible valleys in the Himalaya. Just weeks after their long Alaskan adventure,

Nick and Tim and their small team were trekking into a dizzying lost world at the tail end of the monsoon, plucking off leeches and scrabbling through trackless jungle. That expedition is the reason we're sitting in his tent now. I can't contain my curiosity any longer. I need to hear the story.

Waiting at the head of the Seti Khola valley was their prize, the south-east pillar of Annapurna III. Everyone I know who has seen this line speaks of it in the same terms we reserve for eclipses, wild storms, giant waves. There were photographs around from earlier expeditions to easier neighbouring peaks. As an architecture student, Tim Leach knew a good line. But nothing could prepare them for the real thing. 'When I first saw it,' Nick says to me, 'I thought, for fuck's sake. It was awesome.'

I knew what he meant. Unlike most people, even some of those who have tried to climb the route, I've stood where Nick did thirty years ago, in 1981, at base camp right under the pillar. Unlike Nick, I arrived by helicopter to report on a British team that chose to fly in rather than risk porters on the steep and dangerous ground below the graceful, twisted pyramid of Machhapuchhre. As I peered over the shoulder of the pilot, my words were lost against the noise of the turbine. *For fuck's sake, it's awesome.*

The view from base camp is too foreshortened to get the required perspective on this behemoth. You need some distance – in time as well as space – to see it properly. Seen from a distance, particularly from the south-west, its architecture becomes clear. The pillar sweeps upward for something like two and a half kilometres, with a near-horizontal step in the ridge at half height, around 6,500 metres – a titanic ogee of granite smeared with dazzling white that leads the eye and the heart ever higher until it is lost in the blue. It has its dark side: the piles of rubble scouring its south face and the séracs poised above the start of the spur itself. But its elegance, the faultless appeal of the pillar, makes it at once perfectly beautiful and wholly indifferent.

In Herman Melville's novel *Moby Dick*, Captain Ahab heaped all the malevolence of the world and his own bitter nature on the white whale, yet you couldn't make that mistake with this mountain. Melville's fish was blood and guts. Annapurna is ice and rock. The visceral compulsion is the same. 'Madness!' Ahab's first officer Starbuck complained as his commander descended into obsession. 'To be enraged with a dumb thing, Captain Ahab, seems blasphemous.'

I'd travelled to the Himalaya with Nick before, and I knew something of the story of his attempt on Annapurna III, but once I'd been there, once I'd seen it for myself, I was transfixed. It all seemed so outlandish. What was in their heads as they made the desperate trek in? Not the rage, not the need for vengeance that had driven Ahab, but *something* had put them there. Their subsequent attempt, for those who know of it, is now just an interesting footnote in the history of alpinism, a brilliant effort, the most successful so far, on one of the outstanding unclimbed lines left in the Himalaya.

It was now obvious to me that there was much more to this story than just climbing history – even if, like the mountain, quite what that was might prove too difficult to reach. This was dangerous ground, personal ground, on the corniced ridge between fact and myth. I sat in Nick's tent listening intently while, in Melville's words, he spun me the yarn, and the idea of Annapurna III seemed as real and present as the mountain outside the tent door.

Had Annapurna III been Nick's whale? The towering, adamantine mirror in which he'd seen himself? It seemed to me like an arrival point, a mark of punctuation in the life he'd lived so far. He and Tim had both been at the forefront of a special generation of alpinists, one that revealed a purer form of the game, shedding the fixed ropes and camps of the past, like a moth dragging itself from a hardened chrysalis. Not since the 1930s had alpinism changed so quickly, and at such a cost.

Had Tim and Nick climbed Annapurna III, the achievement would have rested alongside that of Kurtyka and Schauer on Gasherbrum IV, or Prezelj and Stremfelj on Kangchenjunga. Instead they walked away, not just from the mountain, but from alpinism itself. They'd looked deep into themselves and no longer saw the sense in what they were doing. If a life could have a crux, then this was surely theirs.

For Nick, the events on Annapurna III came at the end of a long trajectory that began with his mother's death. Nick was born in Manchester as the eldest of five brothers. His father James worked for a printing company. 'He was a machine minder for almost all his working life,' Nick says. He turns on to his back to stare at the tent's ceiling. 'He hated it. Later on, he did an art course in Leicester and it opened up the world to him. He told me: "Never go and work in a factory." I did, but only to get money to go climbing.'

Nick's youngest brother Simeon was just two when their mother was rushed to hospital, fatally ill with pancreatitis. Nick was ten. 'From the day my mother died,' he says, 'I had to be the responsible person in the family. I had to do a lot of shopping. I had to do a lot of cooking and cleaning. We used to get home help at first, ladies from the local church, that sort of thing. But it soon stopped.'

Some people thought the family should be broken up. A local teacher wanted to adopt Simeon. Their father had to chase off a social worker. The existential threat to his family's autonomy marked Nick more than their poverty did. He likes to tell a story that could be lifted from a tabloid rant about the feckless poor. Looking to distract his sons, James would take the boys for walks on the edge of Manchester, small adventures to escape the drab city streets. One weekend while they sat resting in a quarry, James lit a cigarette and passed the packet to Nick, then a young teenager. Not wanting to be left out, Matthew took one as well, and so on, down the line, until all five brothers were puffing away, to the outrage of passers-by.

James worked in Longsight, a working-class neighbourhood of red-brick houses in a city famous for its rainfall and its brash impatience. The family lived just across the street from the house of Joe Brown, a star of British climbing for two decades, who had torn up its well-heeled social fabric and made it relevant again to the rest of the world. Until he was about fifteen, Nick climbed with his dad and brothers, taking courses in Snowdonia with the Mountaineering Association. Then his dad broke his leg in a fall, and Nick stopped climbing. He became, in his phrase, 'a lad around Manchester', going to the football and turning into a bit of a tearaway.

He got back into climbing through Nick Donnelly and his brother Steve, friends he'd known since his early schooldays. They started exploring for themselves, getting into scrapes down caves or up crags in the nearby Peak District. Nick Donnelly had a mop of blond hair while Nick Colton's was dark, so in the way of these things they became Blond Nick and Black Nick.

'It was a fantastic thing for me,' Nick says. 'I no longer had all that commitment and baggage about my family and looking after my brothers. I'd been bullied at school but was no longer at school. Nobody knew who I was. I wasn't Nick Colton, this scruffy little urchin. I was just another climber. People accepted me. It was liberation. I didn't have any high aspirations or big theories. I was just being myself. For the first time in my life, I was free.'

'When did you become ambitious?' I ask him, almost forty years later.

He purses his lips. 'I'm not sure I ever did.'

'You were with the right crowd?'

'I was with the right crowd. I didn't have any great aspirations.'

Nick climbed with several key British alpinists from that era, but his most famous connection was with Alex MacIntyre. Tousle-haired, bohemian, notoriously unwashed, 'Dirty' Alex dismissed the infrastructure the previous generation left draped on the mountains. 'The wall was the ambition,' he later wrote. 'The style became the obsession.'

'He had a plan,' Nick says. 'He wanted to be good at what he did.'

Today, almost thirty-five years after Alex's death on Annapurna, photographs of him still exude wildness and swagger. He has the aura of a lost rock star, one of those who flew too high then crashed and burned. Even Alex's friends acknowledge he lagged behind on rock climbing ability, but he trained hard and focused on his greatest talents: commitment and daring.

During the winter of 1972, Chris Bonington, Dougal Haston, Mick Burke and Bev Clark attempted a new line on the Grandes Jorasses. A ski-plane flew their equipment and supplies up the Leschaux Glacier, and they spent a fortnight fixing ropes. There was nothing exceptional about their style; this was an era during which Himalayan siege tactics crept into the Alps and plenty of new climbs were done this way. But Nick and Alex saw it as an ethical dead end.

'We had a vision,' Nick says, 'and it was so easy to follow. It came from free-climbing routes in Britain. It was an extension of that into the Alps, and later into the Himalaya.'

In *Mountaineer*, one of his autobiographies, Bonington states that with one more day of good weather his own group would have finished the route. He adds that Nick and Alex completed the line four years later 'in early autumn when the stone-fall danger is reduced'. Bonington's statement is incorrect. It was, as Nick explains, 'the height of summer', and the danger of rockfall was at its highest.

He and Alex climbed the Dru Couloir to prepare themselves. 'I became so tired that somewhere near the top I fell asleep,' Nick says. His gear loop snapped, sending their rack tinkling down the cliff. 'At the summit, Alex said: "That was all right, we'll do something bigger next."' They had a rest day and headed for the Jorasses.

Setting out in the late evening, Nick and Alex soloed from the toe of the Walker Spur to the start of a long, steep ice runnel. After Alex led the first pitch, Nick headed up some hollow ice that had separated from the rock below. Alex belayed from a single tied-off peg. 'I was stood on this detached ice, and the rock above was dusty and loose,' Nick says.

'A handhold snapped, and before I knew it I was flying. I was thinking, fuck, he's on a tied-off peg. We didn't have belay devices in those days either, and the rope was round his waist. Then I stopped.'

There was nothing to say. They'd entered a world of total commitment. Nick climbed back to the belay and completed the pitch. Alex led a second ice runnel and a section of hard black ice that gave way to mixed ground. It wasn't so much the difficulty of the climbing, as its seriousness. They were totally strung out. Finally they reached the long gully spearing down from the top of the Walker. They stopped at a ledge just below the cornice at around six in the evening, less than twenty-four hours after setting out from the hut. Then, with the stove out for a brew, they fell asleep.

'It felt like a real step up,' Nick says. 'The length of the thing: on and on and on. It was the route that crystallised Alex's ambition. He talked about his place in mountaineering. We thought we'd made a name for ourselves having done this big climb. Bonington and that lot had gone past their sell-by date.'

In the red glow of our tent, he laughs, a man now in his mid fifties, his once-black hair now silver-white. 'Wouldn't it be great if we could take those routes that had been done with fixed ropes in siege style and do them without? We identified three, the Desmaison Route on the Jorasses, the Direct Route on the Whymper Spur and the Harlin Route on the Eiger. Those were seen to be the routes that crystallised the old way of looking at things. But it was our time now.'

Even so, they didn't climb together in the Alps again. Nick tried René Desmaison's climb with Gordon Smith instead. High on the face, a flake of rock trapped and broke Smith's foot, and they were forced to retreat. Alex made the first alpine-style ascent of the Eiger Direct with Tobin Sorenson, freshly returned from smuggling bibles into Bulgaria. Perhaps the aura of Messianic zeal surrounding Sorenson chimed more closely with Alex's sense of destiny.

After the Eiger, Alex was pretty much done with the Alps. He had bigger objectives in mind, first in the Hindu Kush and then the Himalaya. He did hard new routes on mountains like Changabang in the Garwhal and Dhaulagiri in Nepal, in the company of the Polish visionary Voytek Kurtyka. Both men had turned their backs on how their contemporaries in their respective countries were climbing. Style really had become the obsession.

'Why didn't you go, too?'

'It didn't occur to me that would be my next step,' Nick says. 'Alex was on a trajectory. I just didn't intellectualise these things. I was with a group of mates and we were having a good time.'

Climbing was about light and escape, like opening a window to a sunny day. It was not about stress or pressure. Even the danger seemed unreal. 'When I was seventeen or so, it felt safer than a football match in Manchester. It wasn't like getting cornered in a street and beaten to bits, which happened. Climbing was just enjoyable.'

By the time he arrived in Nepal in the late summer of 1981, that attitude had changed. Nick was now in his mid twenties and he'd been at it long enough to understand the nature of the game. Even so, the immensity of Annapurna III, its prodigious vastness, must have been a shock. He's staring at the wall of the tent, remembering all this, and then he says simply: 'The commitment was terrible.'

There were just four of them, with Tim's girlfriend Ros Finch and a third climber, Steve Bell, followed by twenty porters. Local people hadn't bothered much with the Seti Khola because the valley was so inaccessible. Consequently, the expedition soon got lost.

After diverting up the wrong valley altogether, the team had to force their way through what seemed like untouched forest. 'Leeches and blood and rain,' Nick says. Above the trees, on a steep open moor below the south face of Machhapuchhre, the badly shod Nepali porters faced a dangerous traverse on steps carved out of rotten rock with an ice axe.

While they did so, they could look straight down into the frothing white of the Seti Khola thousands of metres below. They promptly quit, leaving the climbers marooned halfway up the valley, their objective tantalisingly out of reach.

'Tim was brilliant,' Nick says. 'He was only a young lad, but he negotiated with this handful of young Tamangs who were dressed in sacks, nothing on their feet. These kids said that for whatever our porters were going to get, they'd do it. They kept going, up and down, up and down, until we'd got to base camp.'

Although on Annapurna III Leach was just twenty-three, he'd climbed Gauri Sankar the year before by a committing new route. His experience proved essential as they struggled to get their equipment and supplies to the mountain, to put advance base camp in the safest place at the foot of the spur and to pick a route that might give them a modicum of safety.

Nick's hands are billowing above him as he describes the huge avalanches and rockfalls that swept away gear caches and threatened the climbers. 'It was like looking into hell. Everything [on the south face] was scoured and ripped away for thousands of feet. All the time there were rocks going off to the left and right, all the way up. It was a spooky place.'

The only option was the system of gullies leading up the front of the spur, which for the most part gave straightforward snow and ice, except for a couple of difficult pitches of rock climbing. It was the overwhelming scale that pressed down on them. Steve Bell joined their first two efforts to stash gear and reconnoitre the route, but he stepped back from the final try. He waited at base camp to offer support should the climbers succeed and then have to descend the long and committing east ridge.

With supplies running low, Nick and Tim climbed the lower spur in two days to the large step at half height – the first curve of the ogee. The rock above, leading up to a smaller second step, wasn't hard, and after a couple more days they were established on the upper section of the spur at 6,500 metres, a thousand metres below the summit. The top of the pillar seemed close, but there was still the long summit ridge and an exhausting and protracted descent. They'd marched boldly up to the monster, and now they felt it stirring. They were suddenly, horribly, vulnerable.

Then, during the night, Tim got sick. 'He said it was a bit of gas he'd inhaled,' Nick says. The stream near our base camp is muted. Outside the tent, the light is starting to fail. Nick's voice drops a little. 'I said the game's up, we've got to go down.'

'What did he say?'

'He was resigned to it. When we got down, he said he was glad I'd told him to go down because he couldn't have done it. I don't think he'd have given up like that.' There's a pause, and then he says very firmly, 'I made the decision, not him. I thought at the time, and I think now, and I also think Tim would back me up, he would have kept on going until he died.'

Next morning, I left base camp with a couple of porters to head home early. I had forty miles to cover in two days, but Nick's story kept me occupied. I knew that he'd quit climbing for a while in the early 1980s and I'd often wondered what prompted his decision. I'd assumed it had something to do with the deaths of Alex MacIntyre and Roger Baxter-Jones in 1982. But Nick had just told me that it was after Annapurna III that he stopped.

'I came to feel that I wanted more out of life than just this,' he said. He recalled a scene from one of the construction jobs he'd used to fund his climbing. 'I was working with this really lovely Irish guy in his sixties, and spent a lot of time with him, chatting. He'd talk about the bog in Ireland and I had no idea of what he was talking about. It was a particularly vicious site, in lots of ways, and people treated him like shit. There was racism because he was Irish, and ageism because he was an old man, and I thought, I don't want to end up like that.'

Nick went back to school to get the qualifications he needed to study philosophy at Manchester University. He had got married just before going to Annapurna and he wanted to start a family with his new wife, which they soon did. The deaths of his former climbing partners didn't surprise him. 'People were dying every year.' But they did make him reconsider why he'd been a climber, and why others had. Why Alex had. He came to think that many of them were seeking recognition. To look in the mirror and feel they'd become somebody. 'But it was clear to me that you could just as easily die. The risk was disproportionate to the rewards, as far as I was concerned.'

Nick tried to capture his thoughts in a ten-page essay he wrote not long after Alex died. His conclusion was that competition climbing offered a way for young people to find recognition without risking their lives. Competition, he argued, was already a big part of climbing – 'People used to nick routes off each other.' – but the fascination with risk was 'like religion in its fervour, and just as mistaken.'

'You mean it was like a cult?' I asked him.

'People have a huge range of motivations and the satisfaction from a climb can be incredibly complex,' he told me. 'It's to diminish the activity to say it's about one thing. Where does the risk fit in? For me, climbing isn't about risk. It's something I accept as part of the activity. But it's not a motivating factor at all. It's a much richer thing than that. If I wanted risk, as a boy from Manchester, there was no shortage. I could go and nick a car. Risk was just a by-product.'

I wasn't sure if I believed him. The appeal of Annapurna III, the source of its grandeur, lay in the gravity of its position and the hazards involved. Style, too, the way in which it might be climbed, was essential. Conrad Anker once wrote: 'my hope for this amazing route is that it will be climbed by fair means. If climbing were about finding a solution to an engineering problem it would cease to be an art. Art is the beauty in mountaineering, and our attraction.'

Still, the question remains: how much risk is it worth taking for so beautiful a prize? And if you properly understand the game, if you fully understand your motivation, does that prize justify the risks? Or would you simply no longer want to take them? If you look into the magician's glass and see yourself as you truly are, would you need it any longer? Is that what Nick had done?

Competition climbing carries its own baggage of rules and commerce. By extolling it in his essay, Colton became a pariah to some old-school commentators, a reputation that would dog him far into the future. I considered the idea that Colton had been lured into something that he was too young to understand properly, and then turned on by those who had led him, but I didn't want to put it so bluntly. So I asked him a less definitive question.

'I wonder if older people have a responsibility to younger people to point out the truth of a thing?'

He wasn't falling for that.

'When I was twenty-six,' he said, the age at which he'd gone to Annapurna III, 'I was fucking grown up.' The loss of his mother, the years of helping his dad care for his brothers, of running wild and then working casual jobs so he could climb hard gave him a different perspective to the university crowd he hung out with. Nick knew what he was doing. 'I don't want to make life hard for people,' he'd told me just before we left his tent that afternoon for a cup of tea. 'But sometimes hardships and difficulties make people stronger.'

Even before I left Nepal, I realised I would have to try to track down Tim Leach. Nick had eventually taken up climbing again. After years of teaching, he was now earning his living as the deputy CEO at the British Mountaineering Council. But Tim had simply disappeared, at least as far as the climbing world was concerned. Why? It seemed a mystery to me. Had he reached the same conclusions on Annapurna III as Nick? They hadn't met again after their expedition to Nepal, but Nick had recently been in touch with Tim, and he gave me an email address.

Two months after returning home, I waited in the lobby of a prestigious, multinational architecture practice at the northern extremity of Farringdon in the City of London. It was early evening, and people were leaving for the day. I passed the time leafing through a book about the company's history, recognising several major buildings I'd visited, both in Britain and abroad. On the walls were photographs of glass and stone in elegant proportions that drew the eye. Around me, I felt that tremor of energy you get in a large enterprise with a strong common purpose. They weren't just discovering beauty here. They were making it: ogees to order.

I also felt apprehensive. My only knowledge of Tim, beyond what Nick had told me, was Peter Boardman's account of their expedition to Gauri Sankar. Boardman, whose name and literary reputation is memorialised in the Boardman Tasker prize, cast Tim as an archetype: the tight-lipped Yorkshireman focused utterly on difficult climbs.

'Since I had been going on a succession of expeditions,' Boardman wrote, 'I felt I was losing touch with hard technical climbing. I was aghast when Tim said that routes like *Right Wall* and *Citadel* were "all right". We used to tease him about his descriptive vocabulary and the way he divided the quality of life into five tiers: "superb", "magic", "all right", "rubbish" and "crap". The eight years' difference between us was a climbing generation, and to me Tim seemed very youthful in his black and white judgments.'

The man who greets me is thirty years older, dressed in a crisp white shirt, a little softer round the edges than he appears in climbing photos, but in good shape. He speaks quietly with a polite smile, but I soon realise that he also speaks directly. As soon as we're settled with a beer, I ask him about Boardman's description of him as dour and intense.

He laughs. 'I probably was then.'

Tim's father, George, was a bank manager. His mother Mary taught at a local nursery school in their home town of Guiseley. George was involved with the local Scouts, and it was on a Scout trip that Tim discovered climbing, aged sixteen. He showed an immediate natural aptitude. Hitching back from the crag one day, he got a lift from Dennis Gray, then the general secretary of the BMC and living across the street from Tim, who was soon climbing the hardest routes of the day, and adding his own.

'If you were a good technical climber, and if you grew up in Yorkshire you tended to be, then alpinism was pretty straightforward,' Tim says. 'In my third season, I was soloing the north face of Les Droites, that kind of thing. You had a 'jug' in each hand, so it was about stamina and keeping cool.'

He was barely twenty when he went to Gauri Sankar, his first encounter with the Himalaya, invited by his mentor Dennis Gray, who had almost climbed the peak in 1964, and wanted another try. But Gray had to pull out, and without his mentor, Tim struggled to fit in with his older, more experienced companions.

'We rushed into base camp and I got bad pulmonary oedema. After a week, I was in and out of consciousness. I had to be helped down to a lower camp. I was pretty pissed off with them for not recognising sooner that I was really ill. Pete with his experience and as the leader should have picked up on that.'

After Tim recovered, he climbed with the others for about three weeks, pushing the route in a very demanding style. 'There was a massive, long traverse that took about a week, and by the end of it we were committed to the next bit. It got very stressful. John Barry fell near the top and broke his arm. It came very close to getting out of hand. It was a good experience, but it should have been a group of mates going away, from the same age group with the same ability. It was all quite formal.'

Still, buoyed by their success, Tim put his studies on hold but he chose new routes with the same aesthetic rigor that would dominate his professional life, roping up with friends from his Alpine climbs, like Steve Bell, whom he'd met during his first season, and Nick Colton. Like Alex, Tim had a sense of where the future might lie. It was a vision that harmonised with his chosen profession of architect, of imaginary lines fleshed out in stone, but in this case with total, even deadly, commitment. 'We were consciously coming up with the best game imaginable,' he told me. 'It was a deliberate attempt to perfect alpinism. To make it the best it could be.'

Tim was precociously far-sighted when it came to objectives, and technically brilliant, but he remained cautious. He would never have gone near the Andes, he told me, because while the mountains were beautiful, conditions were so poor it seemed suicidal. Alex was the opposite. 'He was basically necky,' Tim says. 'He put himself in situations where if he pulled it off, it was a fantastic coup.'

That sense of theatre attracts an audience, I think, whereas Tim's brand of cold judgment is usually practised alone.

'Did you want to be famous?' I ask him.

'Respected is the word I would use. I wanted to be respected by my peers. I was never interested in being famous.'

It soon became obvious to me that Annapurna III had been a magical glass for Tim, just as it had for Nick. Recalling many of the same incidents, Tim described the huge flakes of loose granite and blobs of frozen snow that blocked their path on the ridge, and how he had dropped one axe – they were using the legendary Terrordactyls invented by Hamish MacInnes – and broken the pick on the other. Their stories began to intertwine in my head, complementing and amplifying each other, until the moment they decided to abandon their climb.

The night before, Tim had changed the gas cylinder on the stove and stuck it in the bottom of his sleeping bag to keep warm. Then he tucked the cowl of his sleeping bag – just like the one Nick had used on our expedition – over his head. Next morning, Tim woke with a headache. He felt nauseous. When he came to light the stove, he discovered the canister was empty. The stove had leaked. He believes that breathing butane all night, rather than the altitude, left him feeling ill.

'I looked at my axe, and I looked at the dollops of snow stuck to the ridge, and I looked at Nick, and I said, "What do you want to do?" I have a very clear recollection of him saying, "It's your expedition; you make the decision." I found that unnerving. You want someone to make a rational decision, rather than say, you organised it; you sort it out. So I said we'll go down. I don't know why because it was a perfect day.'

This recollection was pretty much the opposite of what Nick had told me. Anyone who has spent time at altitude understands how memories can be distorted. It's plausible Nick said something to Tim he hoped was definitive about going down without sounding critical, and that Tim failed to understand this. It's possible Tim needed to rationalise their failure, which soon became the fracture line in his climbing career. It's equally conceivable that Nick or Tim – or both of them – was already, unconsciously, at work on the narrative. Self-deception is an intrinsic part of human nature. We are consummate liars, not just in a malevolent sense, but also as an unintentional consequence of hunting out comfort, justification, meaning for what we do. It seemed likely to me that both these men looked up and at a visceral level knew death was waiting for them.

How much do these moments change things? Beyond revealing our true natures? For an instant, we recognise we are not capable, or willing. That this is not what we want, that we would rather something else. And that instant of recognition, of revelation, defines us, just as much as the realised dreams do – perhaps more so.

Two things occur to me as Tim tells me his story. Had there been lines of fixed ropes and camps below them, I feel sure the clarity of that crucial moment would have been diminished or even dispelled. It also seems likely, even probable, that their reluctance to push on saved their lives.

'We came down to base camp and it started snowing,' Tim says. 'And it was a massive epic to get out. It reached the stage where if we'd been a day later we wouldn't have got the porters out. I don't know why I made the decision to come down. But it was nagging in the back of my mind. If we'd continued it would have taken us two days minimum, probably three days to get to the top, then it's a very hard descent down the east ridge.'

Tim's life wasn't at the same tipping point as Nick's. He was still only twenty-three. But what he faced on Annapurna III had a similar impact. 'When we got home, I thought to myself, do you want to keep doing this? It wasn't a wholly conscious decision. I thought this is too risky. I need to get back and finish my studies.'

Then the bleak toll of famous names that characterised British alpinism in the early 1980s began. Pete Boardman died in the spring of 1982, along with Joe Tasker on the north-east ridge of Everest. That autumn, Alex MacIntyre was killed by a stone falling from the south face of Annapurna. 'It really was like Russian roulette. You could be in control completely of how you were operating and still die. Look at Alex. It just seemed unsustainable. You can't keep putting yourself in those positions and expect to get away with it.'

Nick continued to turn events over in his mind, attempting to understand them. Tim set a new course. 'It wasn't enough to scale down and do a bit. I had been completely obsessive about climbing. So I decided to do something else. To be an architect.' He sips his beer. 'It was probably a good move.'

Unencumbered by the past, Tim prospered. In the late 1990s, he was responsible for the team that remodelled the Royal Opera House in London, at a cost of £200 million. In Tim's line of work, it would be hard to conceive of a project with more public exposure. I asked him whether the anxiety and doubt he'd experienced on Annapurna III had helped.

'Oh, absolutely. Most of my colleagues are petrified about failing professionally. Of cocking something up. And I think, how bad can it be?

You're not going to die, however embarrassing. Whether climbing teaches you that, or whether you go climbing because of it, I don't know. But climbing did give me the confidence to say, do what you want to do and create the environment in which to do it.'

'Do you miss it?'

'I missed the freedom. But maybe that was to do with how old I was. The one thing I was convinced by, and maybe this is my character, is that if you're going to do something you should do it really well, and if you can't then don't do it. That's perhaps why I dropped out of climbing so quickly and so efficiently.'

'Did you pay attention to it afterwards?'

'No.'

When he started work, Tim says, he carried on rock climbing for a while, but with a new career, he couldn't reach the necessary level of fitness, and he found he no longer felt the necessary drive. So he quit, this time for good. Yet talking about the wild, about mountains, he is still animated. 'If you're interested in the aesthetic, the aesthetic drives you. I've just come back from cycling in Scotland, and I look at the hills and they're just gorgeous. I see a line and I think: I'd love to climb that. The attraction is still there.'

Leaving the pub, we shook hands. Tim headed north while I walked west to the Underground. Before we parted, he said that I should really contact Steve Bell, the third climber on their expedition, for his view. I'd thought that what had happened on Annapurna III was just between Tim and Nick. That moment of decision, the unfolding shape of their lives in the decades since, the beauty of Annapurna III, still unclimbed – these were the things that fascinated me. Yet the discrepancy between their accounts of what happened that morning made me think again.

Perhaps Steve remembered what happened and could offer a neutral perspective? I also knew Steve was living in Australia, so I put the suggestion to one side for later. I left for India on another trip.

A few weeks after my return, I discovered Steve was back in Sheffield to visit the guiding company he part owns. I hadn't seen him for a couple of years, and knew he had suffered ill health, but when we met for lunch he seemed as fit as ever. He explained that while he could no longer shoulder a rucksack, he was cycling and rock climbing a lot near his home at Arapiles. Like Nick and Tim, he had vivid memories of the expedition: how psychologically hard it had been, how committing their location had felt in the days before satellite phones and powerful helicopters. After we'd talked for a while, I told him about Nick and Tim's conflicting memories of the moment they decided to bail. Could he remember anything?

He smiled. 'It's thirty years ago, I'm sorry. I can remember that they both thought it was too much. That's all.'

'I guess you didn't have the same emotional connection to that moment,' I said.

'No, but I did feel very emotional about my decision to pull out.' He had gone part way up the pillar to stash some gear, and he'd realised the objective was too much for him. The climbing was fine, but up above the pillar the ridge stretched on and on, and then there was the descent. It was clear he had made the same decision as Tim and Nick had, only without leaving the ground. In the years that followed, Steve qualified as a guide, and he maintained his connection to the mountains, but when I suggested the expedition wasn't a turning point for him as it had been for the others, he disagreed.

'After Annapurna III, I ceased to be a climbing bum,' he told me. 'I realised I needed to do something else.' When he got back from Nepal, he applied, simultaneously, to university, the Royal Marines and the British Antarctic Survey. After his spell in Antarctica, he served four years in the Marines before setting up his business with Steve Berry.

Nick and Steve Bell had been good friends on the expedition, but Steve had found Tim almost austere in his commitment to the mountains, focused on the prize ahead of him rather than the world around him. When I told him about how contented Nick seemed roaming around western Nepal that spring, he nodded and suggested that was 'the mature approach, the right approach'.

Walking back to his office, we gossiped about mutual friends, but I felt strongly the amount of time that had passed – ninety years between them – since they'd all trekked home from Annapurna III. I thought about the things they'd done and the kids they'd had. The lives they'd led. I thought about the famous photographs I knew of Alex, frozen in time. Annapurna III had been a crisis for all of them, and they'd all responded in different ways. Tim, driven by ambition and his strong sense of the aesthetic, had moved on to a new world that welcomed his intense dedication, seemingly without a backward glance. Nick had pondered the same events, and finally made sense of them and of the world he'd inhabited. Family had always been important to him, and after Annapurna, as a new father, he had plenty to occupy him. These days, it seems to me, he understands what he loves about climbing, and what he needs from it, while remaining extraordinarily open-minded. Steve also built something of lasting value, returning from Annapurna to make the life he wanted.

George Eliot once said that landscape gives the self more room to move in. What if that landscape is yours and yours alone? What if the trail you leave through the frozen kingdom is unique? What couldn't you do after that? The steps these men had taken halfway up this mountain had left a trail of bootprints in their minds they could follow again and again. Never mind that they led nowhere.

No doubt someone will one day climb the south-east pillar of Annapurna III. The next Kurtyka, perhaps, or the next Steve House. I hope they do it in good style. No doubt they will be admired and praised. It had been a year since I had stumbled so awkwardly in Nick's footsteps, a year spent thinking about what he and Tim, and also Steve, had achieved. I remain full of respect for their decision, and for their half-route. They went out and found the line. Then, recognising their limits, they stepped back.

Some mountains are better left unclimbed.

In May 2016, three of modern alpinism's biggest talents, Hansjörg Auer, Alex Blümel and David Lama attempted the south-east ridge of Annapurna III. They reached the same point as Nick Colton and Tim Leach in 1981.

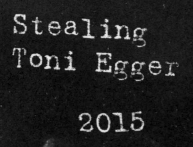

Stealing
Toni Egger

2015

Stefanie Egger struggles to her feet and disappears into the kitchen to fetch something she wants me to see. Now in her mid eighties, Steffi no longer moves easily, but her eyes are bright and her mind is sharp. She's suffered more than many from life's hardships, but this seems only to have whetted her dry sense of humour. Returning to the table, she lays in front of me a photograph taken of her family in 1930 when they still lived across the border in the Italian mountain town of Bolzano – called Bozen by its German-speaking population.

It's a formal family portrait and the children are in their best clothes. Stefanie's mother stands at her husband's shoulder, her right arm resting on the back of his chair. Steffi sits upright on her father's lap while her three brothers group around their mother. Franz, eight years old, is the only one of the brood with even the hint of a smile. Next to him is Hans, two years younger, with full lips and his head tilted to one side, looking a little dreamy. In front of him is the youngest boy, Toni, dressed in a checked wool jacket with a lick of blond hair over his forehead. He looks unusually focused for a child of four.

'Toni was the darling,' Steffi says without a trace of envy or resentment. 'He could do no wrong. *Toni war alles.* He was everything. And if he wanted to be a mountain guide, then that was perfectly fine with my mother.'

While I scan the photograph, Steffi's hand rests on another image, quite possibly the last ever taken of her brother, although this detail, like so much of Toni Egger's last days, is now a matter of intense controversy. The image is taken from Cesare Maestri's book *Arrampicare è il*

Mio Mestiere – Climbing is My Trade – first published in 1961, two years after the two men, as the book claims, made the first ascent of a peak routinely described as the most beautiful and difficult in the world.

Reinhold Messner called Cerro Torre 'a shriek turned to stone', but that's only when the wind blows. Under blue skies and high pressure it's the closest you can imagine to mountaineering perfection, the Platonic ideal of what a climbing challenge should be. It provokes something akin to lust, which might explain that while gorgeous, the peak has borne witness to some morally questionable behaviour. As the famous French alpinist Lionel Terray put it, looking over at Cerro Torre from the summit of nearby Fitz Roy: 'Now there's a mountain worth risking one's skin for!'

Through the 1950s, as ponderous national expeditions were planting flags on the summits of the world's highest peaks, the true prophets of alpinism turned elsewhere to spy the future. Even though Lionel Terray, who had made the first ascent of Fitz Roy in 1952, dubbed Cerro Torre 'impossible', Patagonia looked a lot more like it than Everest. Cerro Torre drew the Italian climbers Walter Bonatti and Carlo Mauri, who made a bold attempt on the tower from the west. It also persuaded Cesarino Fava, an Italian émigré to Argentina, to write to the most famous climber from his home district, the man dubbed the Spider of the Dolomites: 'Come here,' he told Maestri, 'You will find *pane per i tuoi denti* (bread for your teeth).'

Maestri acted on Fava's invitation and when he returned to Italy and a hero's welcome in 1959 after claiming Cerro Torre's first ascent, the world of alpinism was duly impressed. At the age of twenty-nine he appeared to have jumped from being merely very good to reaching a place among the immortals. Terray wrote: 'The ascent of Cerro Torre … by Toni Egger and Cesare Maestri, seems to me the greatest mountaineering feat of all time.' Maestri himself loved making provocative or hyperbolic statements. 'I wished to use climbing as a way of imposing my personality,' he once said. Now, it seemed, he really had something to crow about. 'This is my joy,' Maestri said, responding to the Italian public who had come out to meet him. 'And it helps to ease the pain of the loss of Toni.'

Stefanie Egger remembers those weeks in early 1959 when Toni was in Patagonia attempting Cerro Torre with Maestri – how her mother grew increasingly alarmed at the continuing silence of Toni, who in the past had been such a good correspondent. Stefanie was almost thirty and living in Innsbruck, working in the *konditorei* – the patisserie – of a local hotel, when the call came from her mother to tell her that her brother was dead.

'You can imagine the impact, when a mother gets the message her son had died,' Stefanie told me. 'I think she thought about the possibility already, because it had been such a long time since we'd heard anything. When your child goes to the mountains, you have to consider the possibility.'

Stefanie went home to Lienz to comfort her grieving mother, and so was there when Maestri showed up at the door holding a bunch of white flowers, the colour, as Stefanie reminds me, of innocence and remembrance. Maestri told Stefanie's mother what had happened: that the two men had been retreating in a storm; that Maestri was lowering Egger, who was looking for a bivouac site; that they both heard a rushing sound before an avalanche roared out of the cloud, sweeping Egger off the face and snapping the rope.

'I didn't believe his story,' Stefanie says. 'I believed they reached the top, but I knew there was something wrong with the story because nothing came back. Nothing. Not a sweater. Not his clothes. Not even his passport. Why? Why did nothing come back?'

Maestri attended a mass for Toni on 2 April and afterwards joined a group of Toni's friends in the Rose pub, where he explained the circumstances of Toni's death and promised to give a slide show about the ascent. It never happened and Stefanie hasn't seen him since. (In the 1980s, Egger's climbing club in Lienz invited Maestri, but he claimed his slides had been stolen.) The Egger family – Stefanie, her mother and her surviving brother, Hans – got on with their lives. For the climbing world, Toni became an abstraction, a two-dimensional character whose story was picked over for evidence in the growing controversy about Maestri's claim. Even when Toni's remains were found by the American climber Jim Donini in 1974, in a location well down the glacier that feeds from Cerro Torre and its satellites, Egger remained somehow remote, a handsome face in a black and white photograph from another era. His remarkable climbing career would soon be reduced to one simple question: How did he die?

While Toni Egger faded from view, Maestri's book went through four editions in a decade, his reputation as one of Italy's greatest climbers seemingly assured. And in each edition the caption to this last photograph of her brother, the one Stefanie is now looking at, remained the same: 'Toni Egger on the lower slabs of Cerro Torre.'

For close students of Cerro Torre's troubled history, this photograph has long prompted questions and a vague sense that something, somewhere, is not right, and for one simple reason: it shouldn't exist. When Cesarino Fava, the third member of the Cerro Torre expedition, who only climbed low on the route and waited in camp while Egger and Maestri climbed on, discovered Maestri more dead than alive at the foot of the granite tower, the only evidence Maestri could offer that he and Toni Egger had reached the summit was his word and his story. The only camera with them had been lost with Egger in his fatal fall.

So where had this photograph come from?

Kelly Cordes, in his compelling history of Cerro Torre, *The Tower*, explains how Egger injured his foot approaching base camp, a wound that became infected, keeping the Austrian at base camp for the initial stages of the expedition. While Egger was recovering, Maestri, with Fava in support, fixed the first 300 metres of the route. Then, according to Maestri's account, he and Egger left for the summit. So if Egger fell to his death on the descent, losing the only camera, how could Maestri publish a photograph of Egger on the lower slabs? The short answer is that the photo is of an entirely different mountain.

'We [Patagonia experts] knew the photo wasn't taken on Cerro Torre, as no place Maestri went there resembled the image,' Cordes told me. 'But it could have been anyplace – could have been back in the Alps, elsewhere in the Chaltén massif, who knows.'

Cordes knows that if you are looking for a needle in a haystack, then ask the man who knows the haystack best. When it comes to Cerro Torre and the Chaltén massif, that man is Rolando Garibotti. Born in Italy and raised in Bariloche in northern Patagonia, Garibotti did his first route in the Chaltén range at fifteen years of age. Not only did he write the guidebook to Patagonia, his book is widely regarded as a classic of its genre, underpinned by knowledge and research that is best characterised as relentless. In 2004, the *American Alpine Journal*, where Cordes was then working, published a seminal examination of Maestri's claim titled 'A Mountain Unveiled'. Garibotti's story was so well researched and convincing that for many leading alpinists, doubts about Maestri's possible fraud ended there; it became accepted wisdom that he had lied about summiting Cerro Torre in 1959. Despite the vitriol and anger Garibotti's case provoked from Fava, Maestri and their supporters, it received no factual rebuttal.

Some of those who clung to Maestri's story, more through faith than reason, said that no one could be certain until they repeated

Maestri's route, something no one had managed to do in more than four decades following Maestri's claim. In November 2005, Garibotti joined the Cerro Torre veteran Ermanno Salvaterra and Alessandro Beltrami for the 'second' ascent of Maestri's line. After the ropes that Maestri fixed up the first 300 metres, and the gear cache at what they presumed to be his high point, they found no trace of Maestri and Egger, nothing at all, though Maestri had claimed to have placed around sixty hand-drilled bolts on the terrain above.

Case closed? Not a bit. Garibotti and Salvaterra, according to Maestri, were simply 'sons of bitches'. Even when Maestri's façade seemed to slip in a tense but revealing interview with the French journalist Charlie Buffet, and he veered close to an admission that his claim was false, there were still plenty of old friends in the Italian climbing world prepared to defend him. Most stalwart of all was Cesarino Fava, his old companion, who described Garibotti and Salvaterra as *'bastardi Torquemada'*, a reference to the sadistic Grand Inquisitor of Spain, Tomás de Torquemada.

The tempest of emotion and anger the Cerro Torre story whips up has shown no sign of abating, despite the weight of evidence. In early 2012, Hayden Kennedy and Jason Kruk removed 120 of Maestri's bolts from the 1970 *Compressor Route*, Maestri's strange, largely artificial second effort at Cerro Torre, an ethical blot both on the mountain and Maestri's reputation. Coming down from the mountain, locals met them with fury and threats of violence and the pair was briefly jailed. ('I will fuck you in the ass,' one local shouted to Kruk through the police-car window, 'like you fucked me in the ass!') News of what the North Americans had done – and their arrest – was reported around the world. Some of the local anger sprang from fears that with the *Compressor Route* now a hard free climb, many climbers would no longer come to Patagonia, hurting local businesses. But there was more to it than that. 'Many of the people infuriated by the bolt removal considered it an affront to Maestri,' Cordes says. 'He holds legendary status among many, and thus anything considered an affront to his legacy might cause further backlash.' Resentment at the largely American and British inquiries into Maestri's reputation had become conflated with attempts to restore some majesty to Cerro Torre's headwall.

Even after his book was published in October 2014, Cordes was still nagging at Garibotti to identify the location of what became known as 'the man in the red sweater'. The photo had been cropped in such a way that very little of the background showed; to the casual observer, the location could have been anywhere. Yet despite the paucity of information, in the spring of 2015, Garibotti solved the mystery. 'After many hours studying images of the entire valley,' Garibotti wrote on his influential blog *PataClimb*, 'with the help of Dörte Pietron, we recognized a feature that matched the photo in question. Bingo! Maestri's photo of Toni Egger was in fact taken on the west face of Perfil de Indio, a small tower north of the Col Standhardt, between Agujas Standhardt and Aguja Bífida, on the west side of the massif, the opposite side that they claim to have been climbing on.'

As Garibotti pointed out, in Maestri's various – and often contradictory – accounts of the 1959 Cerro Torre climb, he had never once mentioned going to the west side of the massif. There were reasons why he wouldn't want to, since it was from the west that his great rivals Bonatti and Mauri had attempted the peak. And in all the weeks Maestri spent in Patagonia, the only time not satisfactorily accounted for were the days Maestri claimed to have been on Cerro Torre.

Garibotti's discovery seemed an unarguable explanation for one of the enduring mysteries of the Maestri affair. If Maestri and Egger weren't climbing Cerro Torre in the six and a half days of Maestri's account, then what were they doing? Having found their route from the east too difficult, did they cross to the west side, to look at the route Bonatti and Mauri had tried, the same route that Maestri had disparaged? And placing Maestri and Egger on Col Standhardt made sense of other discoveries: Egger's remains had been found on Cerro Torre's east side, below Col Standhardt, suggesting the climbers had been returning from the west to their base via the col; a curiously knotted rope found with Egger's body suggested a bungled crevasse rescue; and injuries to Maestri's hands and wrists were observed by the small band of students helping supply the expedition. Did Egger fall irretrievably into a crevasse on his way down from the col?

Locating this troublesome photograph was news, so the Italian journalist Sandro Filippini, working for Italy's biggest sports paper, *La Gazetta dello Sport*, called Maestri for a response. Maestri doesn't often welcome journalists, but Filippini had an advantage, having known the old alpinist for years. During a series of conversations, Maestri denied he had ever visited the western side of the Cerro Torre massif; then he said the photo was someone else's and that his editor had captioned it incorrectly; finally he remembered that during his first expedition to Cerro Torre, in 1957/58, he had in fact been to Col Standhardt to 'look at the ice cap' that dominates Cerro Torre's western aspect. Maestri also told Fillippini that the man in the photo was not Toni Egger but Luciano Eccher.

Bruno Detassis was leader of the 1957/58 expedition that gave Maestri his first view of the mountain that would make him famous. But having looked at it, Detassis forbade his climbers from even setting foot on it. The mountain was simply too dangerous. When the expedition returned to Italy, Detassis published a thorough account of their exploration, with a day-by-day diary of where they had been, in several different journals. None of them mentioned going near Col Standhardt. 'Detassis' account leaves no room for Maestri's explanation,' says Garibotti. 'Also, none of the other lengthy literature on that trip [does].' Garibotti also says that even though Luciano Eccher was the expedition filmmaker, there is no other photograph or film footage of such a significant piece of exploration in the expedition records or anywhere else.

Garribotti's meticulous research cut no ice with one section of the Italian climbing community. When the author and mountain historian Mirella Tendirini posted the *Gazetta* story on her Facebook timeline, the comments poured in, many of them excoriating Garibotti and his erstwhile climbing partner Ermanno Salvaterra. Garibotti, they suggested, wanted fame or was jealous. The photo caption was clearly just a minor mistake, nothing more.

'In an era in which conspiracy is king, I'm not surprised there are those who pick out these things,' one climber argued. Tendirini herself wondered what had driven 'Anglo-Saxon climbers' – referring to early sceptics from both Britain and the United States – to pursue Maestri in 'a witch hunt'. She wrote of 'the malevolence and fury, which has accompanied all the accusations during the long quest of most people not of truth but just of proofs to send Maestri to the stake'.

After reading Tenderini's comments, I contacted her. 'I've always had the impression,' she told me, 'that the obstinacy with which the searches have been supported and carried out through [the] decades originated more from an instinctive aversion towards the man rather than from a real desire for clarity and truth. Of course Maestri's attitude did not help, and of course I do not think that all Anglo-Saxon climbers are against Maestri just because they do not like him, but this is the explanation why it's hard for me to remove that early feeling of a persecution being enacted.'

When Garibotti's blog post about the location of the photo appeared, I looked hard at the figure in the centre of the frame, but couldn't tell much about its identity. Although Maestri's photograph is a little indistinct, I noticed that the man in the red sweater – a fashionable colour for 1950s alpinists – also had something white on his head. I showed it to friends and asked them to look, too. They all said the same thing. It's not possible to tell whether this white headgear is a hat or a helmet, but as several climbers from that period told me, the use of climbing helmets only became common in the 1960s. Maestri didn't have one on Cerro Torre. The alternative, a white cap, certainly seems plausible. One of the regularly published photographs of Egger shows him wearing a white cap, and when I met Markus Huber, president of Egger's old climbing club, the Alpenraute Lienz, I asked him about it.

He agreed that the figure was wearing a white cap. Then he told me: 'White caps were a hallmark of our club, like a calling card.' Huber had also studied the photograph and believes the man in the red sweater is Egger. 'Not just from the hat,' he says. 'We have many photographs of Egger in our archive and I have seen him standing just like this, in this position in other photographs. I feel it is him.'

Sitting in a restaurant in Lienz, he brings out some of the Alpenraute's treasures connected to Egger, including his diaries. Stefanie had told me of Toni's stylish handwriting: 'He only went to an Italian school,' she said, 'but he wrote beautifully in German, without mistakes. Where did he learn that?' Keeping diaries began when he started climbing, Stefanie said, as a way of recording his climbs. They are now in my hands and Stefanie is right; the handwriting is beautiful.

Markus opens one of the books at an entry in the summer of 1954. It's an account of Egger's epic day with his good friend Gottfried Mayr, also of the Alpenraute, when they climbed the *Comici* and *Cassin* routes on the north faces of the Cima Ovest and the Cima Grande in an eleven-hour push. Egger had a reputation for climbing fast, so fast that partners would sometimes nag him to slow down and place more pitons. His written account of what was in the mid 1950s a dazzling performance is laconic. He laughs at his own shortcomings and underplays his successes. He is not at all competitive or boastful.

The contrast with Cesare Maestri could not be starker. Maestri loved bombast; he dismissed Terray's assessment that Cerro Torre was impossible. 'Impossible mountains do not exist,' he told supporters who met him in Milan after the climb, 'but only mountaineers who are not able to climb them.' He mocked Walter Bonatti and Carlo Mauri when they named the col on Cerro Torre's southern side the Col of Hope: 'There is only the will to conquer, hope is the weapon of the weak.'

When a group of leading British climbers, having failed on Cerro Torre's supposedly easier south-east ridge, publicly doubted Maestri, he went back to the mountain with a gas-powered compressor and steeplejacked his way up the ridge they had attempted to produce the *Compressor Route*: 'I return and attack their routes,' he wrote, 'the routes they were not able to climb. I will humiliate them, and they will feel ashamed of having doubted me.'

Markus Huber gives a wry smile. 'You don't find anything remotely like [Maestri's bombast] in Toni's diaries,' he says. 'Climbing meant something different to him than it did to Maestri. He didn't do things to be famous.'

The controversy around Toni Egger's mysterious disappearance has to some extent robbed him: of his identity, of his character and even his achievements. Maestri himself has been wildly generous, describing Egger as the best ice climber in the world, who had found climbing Cerro Torre's freakishly iced-up north face 'a Sunday stroll'. Maestri even proposed, with success, that the neighbouring peak be called Torre Egger. But this version of Egger as a superhuman climbing genius has acted as a smokescreen, concealing the truth.

As I listen to Stefanie Egger talk of their childhood, a more human and rounded version of Toni Egger emerges. His story is one of upheaval and exile; climbing gave him a sense of belonging and purpose, freeing him from the shadows of the past. On Stefanie's wall are three family portraits, the first of her great-grandparents in the kind of Tyrolean clothes that are now the stuff of museums. Steffi knew her great-grandfather and remembers him calling for a candle as he lay dying 'to light the way to heaven'.

She and her three brothers grew up on the other side of the Italian border in Südtirol, or as the Italians called it, Alto Adige. Their mother was from Siebeneich, on the road just outside Bozen on the way to Meran. Their father was from Mölten, north-west of Bozen. He was a timber merchant and by the time the war started his two elder sons, Franz and Hans, were working for the family business. The German-speaking population had long been under pressure from Mussolini's fascists to 'Italianise', and wearing traditional Tyrolean clothes like the ones in Stefanie's photograph became a political act of defiance. Mussolini banned education in German, which is why Toni and Stefanie were taught in Italian, despite being native German speakers.

Under a deal struck between Mussolini and Hitler, German speakers could either relocate to the Third Reich or stay where they were and continue to face harassment. Many ended up in western Poland, but in 1940 the Eggers moved to Osttirol and the outskirts of the medieval town of Lienz, where Toni's father rented land and switched to farming. Their nationality would continue to be a vexing issue. Stefanie counts off on her fingers how her legal status changed in the course of the war: 'Italy, Ostmark, Reich, then "without state", then Italian again, then Austrian.' For the latter status, Stefanie had to pay the new Austrian government 3,000 schillings, around five months' salary. Toni Egger is correctly described as Austrian, but he had grown up on the same side of the border as Cesare Maestri.

Stefanie was only eleven when the family moved to Austria, and so she had some education in Lienz, although, she says, 'there was too much *Heil Hitler!* and propaganda. I learned nothing.' Her brother Franz was drafted into the army, and she remembers the telegram arriving saying he had been killed in action fighting in the savage confrontation at Monte Cassino in Italy. It was 24 March, her brother Hans's birthday. That same day Toni was sent his call-up papers. Their father, who never got over losing his eldest son, died of a brain tumour the following year. Toni saw out the war in France, posted to an airbase in the Ardennes. As Egger himself told friends, the only time he was ever frightened was running around the corner of a trench and coming face to face with an American soldier. Both men carried machine guns. Neither man fired and Toni escaped unharmed.

Stefanie can remember clearly Toni's sudden passion for climbing, something no one else in the family shared. 'A girlfriend and I wanted to go dancing,' she says. 'My mother said we could go if we had a chaperone. So Toni came dancing, too. He was just back from an internment camp [after the war]. He had to learn to dance too.' She continued, 'He always protected me. My older brothers wouldn't take me with them but Toni would bring me along. Franz and Hans would complain about that. Then one day he said, "I can't come dancing tonight, I'm going climbing." That's when he joined the Alpenraute.'

Markus Huber has trawled the club's records for details of Toni's early climbing career. 'From the beginning he was a very talented climber,' he says. Long-armed, even gangly, but otherwise physically unremarkable, he was psychologically strong and entirely at home in the mountains. 'I'll marry in sixty years,' he would say, 'when I've finished climbing.' His first climbs were in the mountains above Lienz, particularly the Roter Turm, where he added several new routes with his friends Hans Sauschek and Andreas 'Heini' Heinricher from Kugach in Carinthia. Toni took Stefanie to the Roter Turm in 1946 on her seventeenth birthday to show her his new kingdom. She enjoyed it, she says, 'But when I looked down I became dizzy.' Just a few months after Toni's death,

Heinricher would die in a climbing accident together with the boy he was guiding, an accident that traumatised the town.

Toni was soon climbing further afield in the Italian Dolomites, sneaking over the border along smugglers' routes through forests to avoid checkpoints. Despite Maestri's assertion that Toni Egger was the greatest ice climber in the world, he spent most of his career on hard rock climbs. Egger repeated many of the testpieces from the pre-war period, routes like the *Solleder* on the Civetta and the *Cassin* on the Piz Badile in the Bernina. He soloed the north face of the Cima Grande in four hours and repeated Gaston Rébuffat's route up the south face of the Aiguille du Midi above Chamonix just two days after the first ascent. As a stateless person after the end of the war, he had no passport to get out of or back into Austria. In 1951, he became a mountain guide, training in Tyrol's Zillertal and earning extra income as a forester in Switzerland.

Egger's professional life prospered too; he moved to the ski town and state capital, Innsbruck, eventually becoming director of a climbing school. In Innsbruck he was invited to join an Austrian Alpine Club on an expedition to the Cordillera Huayhuash, to attempt the first ascent of Jirishanca, dubbed 'the Matterhorn of the Andes'. (The leader of the expedition was the novelist and political activist Heinrich Klier, who in the 1960s joined the South Tyrolean Liberation Committee, an organisation campaigning for the rights of German speakers by blowing up Italian fascist memorials.)

By any standard this was a hugely successful expedition. The team went on an orgy of first ascents in the Cordillera Raura, both before and after climbing in the nearby Huayhuash. And when snow conditions on Jirishanca proved dangerous, Egger and Siegfried Jungmair took themselves off to Yerupajá Chico, making a three-day ascent of its north-east buttress and east ridge, a nervy climb up rotten limestone, dodging rockfall and avalanches and overcoming a final difficult ice ridge.

Jirishanca itself proved even harder; the team said afterward it was the hardest climbing they'd encountered anywhere. Climbing to Camp 2 was easy enough for it to be supplied by porters, but after that the climbers faced vertical limestone and a huge overhanging cap of ice they were forced to tunnel through. Above that was a second buttress that was even harder, leading to a final snow and ice ridge up to seventy degrees. It was the poor condition of this ridge that persuaded them to take a break at the end of June and retreat down their fixed ropes.

Two weeks later they were back to finish the job, traversing the remaining six pitches to the summit on the north face because the cornices were so bad. They reached the top in a storm. Nick Bullock also climbed a new route on Jirishanca's south-east face in 2003, called, appropriately enough, *Fear and Loathing*. 'I can still remember how out there we were and how at the time Al Powell and I considered the east buttress in 1957 was such a years-ahead-of-its-time ascent,' Bullock said. 'The mountain is moody; it attracts bad weather when all the others around are bathed in sun. Being high on that east ridge certainly feels committing, and very spectacular.'

The routes on Jirishanca and Yerupajá Chico were among the hardest yet done in the Andes, according to the *American Alpine Journal*. And Cesarino Fava often said that Egger told him he thought Cerro Torre would be no harder than Jirishanca. Yet the comparison is a false one. It took Egger and Jungmair most of their summit day to cover six pitches, around 300 metres on ground less steep than any theoretical ice sheet on Cerro Torre's north face. The tragedy of the Cerro Torre fraud is that Egger's impressive ascent of Jirishanca, hailed at the time, has faded from view against the drama and circumstances of his death. Maestri didn't just steal the first ascent; he stole something of Egger.

You may wonder, almost six decades years after Egger's death and after Maestri's story has been shown so thoroughly to be mendacious, why Maestri, at the time of writing eighty-six years of age and increasingly frail, needs to tell the truth. 'Morally,' Rolo Garibotti argues, 'someone who lied for personal gain about the circumstances leading to the death of his partner should not be given a free pass on the grounds of him being an important pillar of a certain community, or on the grounds of his age. No matter which moral compass you use, his behaviour in relation to Toni Egger's family and friends was [and] is disgraceful.'

'It's important because the truth matters,' Kelly Cordes says. 'Liars undermine those who conduct themselves honestly, and deny them opportunities. Furthermore, with 1959 on Cerro Torre, there remains an unexplained death. I defy anyone to argue that Toni Egger's life and death are unimportant.'

Stefanie Egger says she has no interest in her country's authorities opening some kind of inquiry into how her brother died. She just wants him to rest in peace. Even if there was an inquiry, under Austrian law, it's unlikely any charges would survive the statute of limitations. But she wants to know how her brother died. 'It would be the greatest present to know the truth,' she concludes. 'My neighbour says she can't understand why it still hurts. When I think about my mother or father, it doesn't bring pain. But when I talk about Toni, it still hurts.'

She hands me a note from the man who was, as far as she knows, with her brother when he died. It had been written the week before my visit, and was the first contact she had had from either Maestri or Fava since the mid 1980s, when Fava had come to visit. It was simply a greeting and told her nothing.

'What do you think happened to your brother?' I ask.

'The man in Campiglio,' she says, meaning Cesare Maestri, 'only he knows. And he doesn't want to say.'

Then she pauses for a moment. 'But I want to know. Before it's too late.'

Searching for
Tomaž Humar

2010

Tomaž Humar warned it would be tough to find him. Even so, just ten minutes after the Swiss rescue team reached the vast south face of Langtang Lirung, a 7,227-metre Himalayan monster, its leader Bruno Jelk spotted a body through the helicopter's window. There was low cloud sitting on Langtang's summit. Humar wasn't where they expected him to be, nor at the right altitude. Yet there he was, in the middle of the steep south-west face at 5,500 metres. It was the morning of Saturday 14 November, 2009. The Slovenian had been there since the previous Monday and Jelk saw at once he was dead.

Even before he achieved fame with his daring solo climb on the south face of Dhaulagiri, Tomaž Humar was a magnet for attention – and trouble. Wildly charismatic, people found him either inspiring or infuriating. His fame spread around the world like a brush fire, taking him far beyond the brilliant but obscure world of Slovenian mountaineering. He consulted astrologers and said the mountains spoke to him. Was he genius, or madman?

Then, like Icarus, Humar found himself plunging back to Earth. Millions of people watched him survive a very public epic, marooned for days on Nanga Parbat, saved only by the selfless courage of a Pakistani helicopter pilot. After that, he was gone, leaving just a hint of his famous smile. From being a headline, Tomaž became a rumour. On Langtang Lirung he was completely alone; he told almost no one what he was doing or where he had gone. Now, however, the whole world knew the Slovenian daredevil was once again in trouble.

With Humar located, Captain Sabin Basnyat banked his Ecureuil AS 350 B-3 and brought it into land at a dirt strip ten kilometres south-east of the mountain. Here a second helicopter was parked, also flown up that morning from Kathmandu with extra fuel and equipment and piloted by Suman Pandey, boss of charter company Fishtail Air. The strip was scratched out of a flat, gravel plain a few hundred metres east of Kyanjin Gompa, a shabby collection of lodges built in the last decade or so round an older Buddhist monastery to serve the thousands of trekkers who head up this valley each autumn.

Kyanjin Gompa is also last call for anyone heading to Langtang Lirung's base camp, although not many climbers head this way. The mountain hasn't been climbed since 1995 and it's easy to see why. Its huge south-east face is threatened by an ugly band of séracs. Its east ridge, route of the first ascent, is long and dangerous. The west ridge is long and technical. The south – more accurately the south-east – ridge divides the mountain's vast south face, and has also been climbed. Either side are kilometres of steep glaciers and steeper walls. A British expedition leader who tried the south-west face in 1980 told me: 'It's very serious, a hell of a long route, hard mixed climbing in between steep glaciers and scree.'

Waiting at the airstrip with Suman Pandey was Humar's friend Jagat Limbu, his regular cook and base camp supporter from previous adventures, and a small group of Sherpas. Most of them had flown up three days before in the same helicopter on an earlier rescue effort. That day the weather had been perfect, but none of them had seen Humar, mostly because they were looking in the wrong place. Even if they had spotted the Slovenian star, there was nothing they could have done to reach him.

The difference this time was the Swiss mountain guide Simon Anthamatten. Three days before, he'd been at home in Zermatt, his gear barely unpacked after returning from his own expedition to Nepal. Anthamatten is a strong alpinist himself, in 2009 winning a Piolet d'Or, sometimes dubbed alpinism's Oscars, for the new route he climbed with Ueli Steck on the north face of Tengkangpoche in Khumbu. He got a call that Wednesday evening from rescue expert Gerold Biner, flight operations manager at Air Zermatt, asking if he'd join a rescue in Nepal. Next morning he was on a flight to the Gulf en route for Kathmandu.

Anthamatten is one of a dozen guides Zermatt's rescue services can call on for emergencies. He's used to being dropped on the end of a line to climbers in distress. No one in Nepal had that kind of experience. No rescue like the one he was contemplating had ever been performed in Nepal – or anywhere else in the Himalaya. The helicopter itself, the workhorse of Alpine rescue teams, had only been in the country for three weeks.

Soon the B-3 was back in the air, with just Basnyat, his Swiss co-pilot Robi Andenmatten and Simon Anthamatten on board. With fewer bodies in the back they could manoeuvre closer to the site of the accident so Anthamatten could judge how best to approach the rescue. Humar had fallen five days before, on Monday 9 November. Anthamatten knew Jelk's judgment was likely correct; no one had expected him to still be alive. But the rescue team felt they had to try.

Back at the airstrip, the crew fixed a twenty-five-metre length of static line to the helicopter and Anthamatten clipped in the other end. Basnyat had no experience of this kind of operation, with a man hanging beneath his aircraft, so he handed control to Robi Andenmatten. There was no way Anthamatten was going up otherwise. Bruno Jelk watched the helicopter and its cargo head back down the valley towards Langtang. It crossed the col on the peak's south ridge and disappeared from view.

Almost at once, Anthamatten was once more with Humar, this time hanging free in space. The body was lying on a relatively flat snow-covered ledge on a steep rock spur. The pilot was able to inch forward until Anthamatten was standing on the mountain. He unclipped and radioed the pilot he was off the line. The helicopter drew back a short distance to let him work.

Humar was clearly dead, and in Anthamatten's estimation had been for some time. 'His first call was on the Monday,' he told me. 'In the call he said he would die. It was soon after that, for sure.' Apart from that, the circumstances of his death were a mystery. 'The way the body looked, he couldn't have fallen more than fifty metres. We have experience of this in our mountains. Somebody falls 300 metres then they lose boots, everything is ripped off and so on. Tomaž doesn't look like this.'

Two things didn't add up for Anthamatten. First, there was the location of the body. According to Jagat, Humar had called him a week before, on 8 November, at 6,300 metres on the mountain's south ridge. This is where the Sherpa team had gone to look for him. But Humar was much lower, at 5,500 metres, in the middle of the south-west face. In his next calls, after the accident, he didn't mention this, just that he would be hard to find. What was he doing there? 'The problem is nobody knows what he was trying to do,' Anthamatten said. 'Maybe he rappelled from the south ridge on to the south-west face and traversed. There's a glacier there.'

Even more confusing was the lack of gear. Humar was dressed, and wearing a duvet jacket, but that's about all he had with him. 'I couldn't find any rope,' Anthamatten said. 'I couldn't find his backpack. He had no crampons on. He had no harness on. There was nothing. Two days before it snowed almost a foot, but it couldn't cover all the gear.' Anthamatten had time enough to look. Having rigged the body with slings he carried on his harness, he called in the helicopter and clipped Humar to the line. Then he waited for ten minutes while Robi Andenmatten flew the dead Slovenian back to the airstrip. 'Something went wrong but we don't know what.' He paused, to think about it some more. 'I have no idea.'

That Tomaž Humar should leave life in a swirl of mystery and headlines came as no surprise to his friends. His biographer, Bernadette McDonald, told me how, when she was researching her book, he could never tell a story straight. 'He'd come at everything from an angle,' she said. 'He would tell stories like they were parables, with a hidden meaning. I'd sit there afterwards wondering, what did he mean by that? It was infuriating.' Despite that, McDonald clearly liked him. 'He had a big heart, like the south face of Dhaulagiri, I always thought, big and complicated and dangerous.'

Complexity – and contradiction – lies at the centre of Humar's compelling story. He was part showman and part mystic, anxious for recognition but reluctant to conform. He could speak about spirituality and his inner eye, and drive around in a sponsored car emblazoned with his own image. When he had a project to sell, he was king of the world, but when things went wrong he could disappear without trace. After the Nanga Parbat rescue, when the journalists he courted were desperate to reach him, he just switched off his phone and took his kids fishing. It seemed the image of himself he had created had started to consume him.

Humar wasn't alone among top climbers in having a big ego. They come in handy at 8,000 metres, when the only thing left to keep you going is ambition. And in the end, it was Humar and not his critics who paid the biggest price. But the arc of Humar's career as an alpinist reveals more than one man's desire to be famous or successful. It's also the story of a young nation coming to terms with change. It's also the story of modern alpinism and its fraught relationship with the media, which it both needs but often despises.

On a snowy day in early February, three months after Humar's death, I walk into a sleepy bar in the picturesque town of Kamnik, a short drive into the hills from Slovenia's capital Ljubljana. Kamnik has produced lots of good climbers, including Humar, and I'm sitting across the table from another, Marko Prezelj. To many hard-core alpinists, Prezelj is the real deal. Some would say he's a more deserving recipient for the plaudits heaped on Humar. Judging by his pronouncements on the subject of fame, however, he doesn't care. 'In Slovenia,' he once wrote, 'fame has the same word as a woman's name: *Slava*. Old people used to say: *Slava je kurba!* Fame is a bitch. One day she is sleeping with one and the next day with another.'

Prezelj, who works as a mountain guide, is in formidably good shape for a man of forty-four. He's also formidably direct about Humar. 'Tomaž was really skilled with the media,' he says in idiosyncratic but fluent English. 'He would say before he went, "If I do this climb it will be like landing on the moon." And because he said so, people believed him. As personalities, we are totally different. I believe he did things because he liked his public profile and liked the attention.'

Prezelj introduces me to a novel English phrase of his own devising: 'tasty talking'. 'You talk nice so the other person will like you or what you're saying. I think you say "sugar-coating". General American population, they like to tasty talk. But I don't think alpinism and tasty talking go well together. Bullshit is bullshit.'

You could argue that what Prezelj dubs tasty talking is just consideration for others – good manners, even – and that his straight talking is prompted more by envy than honesty. When I suggest he envied Humar's fame, he nods and smiles. 'Maybe at a certain time in my climbing life I found this frustrating. I felt that what I was doing wasn't recognised. People didn't understand the difference between what I was doing and what others were talking about.'

Prezelj had a long association with Humar. Four years older, he saw Humar arrive as a rookie, followed his progress, knew his foibles and then watched from a distance while his charismatic rival became a national sporting hero. 'He was always very energetic,' Prezelj says. 'But now, looking back, I can see that from the start he was looking for recognition.

I remember once, when we were very young, walking through town and seeing him cycling towards me on his bike very quickly. He saw me and was shouting, "What's the time? What's the time?" He wanted me to see him, to see that he was racing, pushing limits.'

If Humar thrived on attention, then the timing of his success, just as Slovenia found its feet as a nation, turbocharged his rise to fame. It's hard to appreciate Humar's impact without understanding how Slovenia and its climbing culture changed in his lifetime. Stroll through central Ljubljana and its history is in front of you. Baroque churches from the era of the Austrian Empire stand alongside utilitarian concrete boxes from socialist Yugoslavia. The newest buildings are more striking, strongly individualistic and obviously more expensive than their greyer neighbours. Slovenia's economy has surged since independence from Yugoslavia and incomes are closer to those in Western Europe.

It's a common error to think of Yugoslavia, a former socialist federation of autonomous republics, as under the influence of the Soviet Union and locked behind the Iron Curtain. In fact, as former citizens enjoy reminding visitors, Yugoslavians were in some ways freer than Americans, certainly when it came to travel. 'We could go anywhere in the world,' says Viki Grošelj, one of the stalwarts of Slovenian mountaineering in the 1970s and 1980s. In his mid fifties, with a trimmed white goatee, Grošelj's grandfatherly appearance is belied by his restless energy. He can't sit still. 'We used to joke that our passport on the black market was more expensive than an American passport. We didn't have much money, but that's another story. The old system wasn't so bad for all of us. Our healthcare system was better because it was free, whoever you were. Everyone was treated the same, whether you were from the street or a big politician.'

He is, understandably, proud of his nation's record in Himalayan climbing. 'In terms of new routes we can compete with the Polish, or whoever, but we have only a tiny population, just two million. This is some kind of miracle.' Grošelj climbed ten of the 8,000-metre peaks, before abandoning the project to raise his family. 'That achievement,' he says carefully, 'was quite interesting in the 1980s.' He now spends his time working as a high-school athletics coach; he also presented a series of fourteen documentaries about the 8,000-metre peaks for Slovenian television. Grošelj's cameraman is Stipe Božič, an old friend who served as Humar's base camp manager on Dhaulagiri. Grošelj says Humar had approached him first to do the job, but Grošelj turned him down. When I ask him why, he pauses.

'I got to know Tomaž well in 1995 on Annapurna,' Grošelj says. 'After that we became quite good friends. But he had two sides. He could be extremely kind and gentle, but also extremely possessive to those closest to him. He wanted them to adore him. When he asked me to come to Dhaulagiri I thought about it, but it wasn't my way. He loved to be the centre of attention. That public attention helped him make big climbs. This is the opposite of my philosophy. I want total peace. I don't even want to think about my family. He enjoyed that everybody knew everything about him. That's not to say that's bad. If it helped, why not? It's not against the law. But it made people jealous.'

Like the brash new buildings in downtown Ljubljana, Humar's dazzling Slovenian charisma pushed Yugoslavia's greyer utilitarian past into the background, if only as far as the general public were concerned. They knew a little about Yugoslavia's past mountaineering triumphs, but those stories featured large teams of grim-faced men who rarely made much connection with the public. They espoused the qualities of a now-defunct social structure. Here was a mountaineer for a new age – of wealth, individual freedom and celebrity.

Tomaž Humar wasn't the first Slovenian climber to blaze his own trail. Ten years before Dhaulagiri, Tomo Česen, a gifted climber with a couple of siege-style expeditions behind him, claimed a new route on the north face of the rocky 7,700-metre peak Jannu, in eastern Nepal, climbed solo. The international climbing world was impressed. In 1990, he announced an even greater achievement, the solo first ascent of the vertiginous south face of Lhotse, Everest's neighbour and among the most impressive challenges remaining. The climbing world went crazy.

It would be hard to overestimate the impact this climb had. Almost nothing in climbing history compares to it. The cream of world alpinism had attempted this face. The great Polish climber Jerzy Kukuczka had died on it. No one had tried it alpine style, let alone solo. And now an almost unknown Slovenian had apparently strolled up it. The biggest names in climbing queued up to meet the taciturn Česen at festivals around the world. Reinhold Messner anointed him as his heir apparent. Some climbers were uneasy at the lack of photographs and his vague route description. But back home in Slovenia, Česen became a national celebrity, suddenly more powerful than the anonymous apparatchiks who, up until then, had governed the direction of Slovenian mountaineering.

Most influential of these was Tone Škarja, who is waiting for me at the headquarters of Slovenia's national mountaineering association Planinska zveza Slovenije, or PZS, in central Ljubljana. He ushers me into a meeting room. Škarja, when we meet, has been a climber for more than fifty years, joining the same Kamnik climbing club as Prezelj and Humar in 1956. He has been a driving force in Slovenian Himalayan climbing for decades, leading important expeditions, and helping develop several generations of mountaineers. This *éminence grise* slides a yellow booklet across the table, detailing every Himalayan expedition involving Slovenians since the first in 1954. Among the many significant first ascents I spot, is a difficult variation on Everest's west ridge, climbed in 1979. The leader of that expedition was Tone Škarja.

Not surprisingly for a man who has led the expeditions section of the PZS for decades, Škarja is a shrewd – and tough – politician. He's been retired from his job as an electrical engineer for twelve years, but he looks lean and fit, and is still handsome. He first encountered Humar at their climbing club and like everyone else who ever met him, was struck by the young man's energy and charm. 'Everybody who met him loved him,' he says. 'He was a young boy then, a great speaker. He had a special talent for communicating. The director of my electrical company told me that when Tomaž asked to see him about his next expedition he decided that Tomaž wouldn't get any money out of him. But when they met, he changed his mind.'

Škarja is justifiably proud of the decades of volunteer service he has given the PZS and talks respectfully about legends from the past. When I bring up the name of Tomo Česen, however, he smiles in a way that says to me: 'This is complicated.' After a moment's thought, he says: 'Maybe one day we will sit down and talk and I will ask him about Lhotse. Before I die. Unofficially, my position, my opinion, is that he didn't climb Lhotse. Officially?' And he runs his finger down the list of Slovenian climbs. Česen's name is still there, with the date of his Lhotse expedition. As far as the Slovenian establishment is concerned, Tomo Česen is still in the fold.

'We all know what happened on Lhotse,' Viki Grošelj says, 'but nobody wants to talk about it any more. We all know he cheated. He had an intentional plan to con the world. I'm sad about that. Because my biggest wish is that Slovenians do this face.' Grošelj tells me a little about his own expedition in 1981 to Lhotse's south face where he injured his back. 'They said I was jealous of him, but we were totally different, from different generations. I was a classic climber; he was part of the new generation of brilliant climbers. I could never be so strong in head or body to do Lhotse's south face. But this [Česen's story] wasn't good for any of us.'

Grošelj has an intimate connection to the Česen controversy. Česen borrowed a photograph belonging to Grošelj, taken on an earlier expedition to Lhotse, and allowed it to be credited as his own. It could only have been taken from near the top of Lhotse and provided clinching evidence to contradict those doubting Česen's claims. Then Česen made a fatal error. In front of a television camera, and with Grošelj looking on, he opined that he didn't think Grošelj's plan of climbing the 8,000-metre peaks was a worthwhile project. Grošelj might agree with him now, but at the time Česen's judgement hurt. Within days, Grošelj revealed that the photo taken high on Lhotse was his, not Česen's, and arguably the greatest achievement in the history of high-altitude mountaineering crumbled to dust.

Although Grošelj says Slovenian mountaineers no longer believe Česen, it really depends on which generation of Slovenian climbers you talk to. One Slovenian star of the 1980s, now in his fifties, told me how he and his climbing partners were amazed Česen could claim the routes he did without apparently training for them. They found him aloof, not a team player. But those from the next generation, including Tomaž Humar before his death, are less certain. Humar never publicly doubted Česen's claim, simply saying that he wasn't there, and that Česen was 'something special'.

Marko Prezelj takes a similar line: 'There's no proof he did it and there's no proof he didn't. So, to me, as long as he says he did it, I believe him. Almost every alpinist in the world has something they did without proof. So if I start disbelieving him, I'd have to start disbelieving others. Besides, I know Tomo, and it helps me to believe, because he's a really special person who is able to do such things. Ultimately, whether he did it or not is not my problem.' Then Prezelj laughs, before adding: 'He didn't do it for me.'

Lhotse was Česen's last Himalayan peak. Now fifty, he runs Slovenia's sport-climbing association and has a good reputation as a rock climber. His sons, Ales and Nejc, are two of Slovenian brightest young alpinists. When Česen championed sport climbing, political wrangling to restructure the PZS brought him into conflict once again with Tone Škarja. 'We fought a bit when they wanted to change everything,' Škarja says.

'But they didn't get it all their way. Now we collaborate officially. It's not friendly, but we work together. We work out our problems, as we did with Tomaž.'

Like Česen, Humar's bold solo climbs appealed to the public. Here was a feisty young talent taking on an out-of-touch, fusty establishment. See what you can do, he seemed to say, when you abandon the old, pre-independence ways of doing things. Your fate is in your own hands. It was an attitude in tune with the times. But it was Tomo Česen who was first to strike out on his own, even before Yugoslavia collapsed. Marko Prezelj sees Česen as Slovenia's first climbing businessman, who was, in his colourful phrase, 'a cockerel who called too early'. Česen, for many a false prophet, cast a long shadow in Slovenia. But he showed there were other paths to follow.

Many young climbers in the West struggle to fund their habit. But they manage. They drive nails, wait tables, or rappel buildings on maintenance contracts, whatever it takes. As long as they've got the cash, they can choose for themselves where they go and what they do. If they fail, then it's not the end of the world. They just lick their wounds, find another job and start again. Most age out and get steady jobs, a tiny minority make it their career.

That's how things are now in Slovenia, but not when Tomaž Humar was born, in a hospital in Ljubljana on 18 February, 1969. His father, Max, worked in construction in a nearby factory and for neighbours, essentially on the black market. His mother Rosalija worked in a shop. They were observant Catholics, saying grace both before and after dinner. Spare weekends were spent on the ancestral farm, where friends and neighbours would gather on Saturday nights to share a bottle of homemade schnapps and sing the old songs. It was a frugal way of life, predicated on hard work and co-operation. Although they could rely on regular wages, free schools and healthcare – and whatever they could get on the side – the Humars were not materially wealthy. Humar told Bernadette McDonald that when he was given the job of feeding the pigs, he would wrap his feet in old bed sheets before putting on his rubber boots. Socks were for school and church.

Even from a young age Humar felt different to his parents and siblings. Hard work he could manage. He was working on construction projects with his father from the age of six, fetching timber and cement. ('What are children for?' his father Max asked.) When engaged, he was a whirl-wind of activity, his energy almost infectious. But the close – and closed – horizons of his parents' lives chafed at an inherent need for freedom. He needed more room to breathe than he found at home.

When his interest in climbing sparked and flared, his parents were bemused. Climbing was utterly pointless and actively dangerous. Why, when life was already hard enough, would he want to put himself – and them – through all that stress and anxiety? As Humar reached adult-hood, the tension with his equally stubborn father only got worse. There were rows about the money he spent on climbing, fury when he wrecked the family car and, worst of all, Tomaž's traumatic and degrading experi-ences during his compulsory spell in the Yugoslavian army.

Humar's months as a conscript in the Yugoslavian army (JNA) changed him. Few mountaineers like being ordered around, and if his parents couldn't make him conform, what hope for his JNA superiors? But the mindless brutality and injustice was intolerable to Humar. His unit was sent to Kosovo, the disputed Balkan territory trapped between Serbia and Albania. As Slobodan Milošević turned the screws of oppression, ethnic Albanians resisted, often violently. Humar, serving in a corrupt and morally bankrupt army, hated what the Yugoslavian leader was doing.

Even worse, when Humar completed his term of service, his command-ing officer ordered him to stay. Twice Humar deserted. He hid in a refuse

dump, was discovered, and sent to a hellish detention centre in Mace-
donia. He tried to escape again, jumping into the Vardar river. Returned
to his unit in Kosovo, he was finally released on the streets of Podujevo,
a mostly Muslim town, dressed in rags, half-starved, sick, and carrying
an unloaded Kalashnikov. Locals stared at the fair-skinned northerner,
but far from threatening him, an Albanian man drove him to the station,
where the ticket-seller took pity, and gave him a free trip home. 'Before
the army,' he said, 'I was an unusual guy. The army made me more unusual.'

Against this backdrop of civil war and economic collapse, as Yugoslavia
spiralled into chaos and then disintegrated, Humar's new passion for
climbing bewildered his family. Even in functioning societies, parents are
puzzled, even alarmed when their child starts climbing. Marko Prezelj's
certainly were. Prezelj tried to balance the need to plan for his future
with his burning passion to be in the mountains, climbing. He studied
chemical engineering at the University of Ljubljana, finally completing
his four-year course after nine years' trying. Like Humar, he came under
pressure to give up his freewheeling lifestyle and knuckle down. 'The rest
of society saw me as a rebel,' he said. Both men found refuge from the
tension in their lives among their friends in the local Kamnik climbing
club. It met each Thursday night to plan that weekend's adventure;
that Thursday meeting was an almost religious obligation. 'The club
was so important,' Prezelj says. 'Those people were like my tribe.' Humar
described the club meetings as Holy Thursday.

In the mid 1980s, before the collapse of socialism, Slovenia's clubs
were the backbone of climbing. Equipment and transport were luxuries
few could afford, so clubs were essential to share resources. They were
also the gatekeepers for reaching the Himalaya. If you couldn't get
along with people, you wouldn't join the major leagues. 'When I started,
there weren't any phones, let alone cell phones,' Prezelj told me.
'We would meet at the club, decide what we wanted to do that weekend
and stick to it.'

Gear may have been rudimentary and cash limited, but Prezelj and his friends were dedicated and focused. In his first full year of climbing, he says, aged eighteen, he went out forty weekends. By the time Tomaž Humar started climbing and joined the Kamnik club, Prezelj had been at it for five years and must have seemed to Humar the established young star. That year – 1987 – Prezelj joined his first Himalayan expedition, to Lhotse Shar, with some of the biggest names from the previous generation.

Humar meanwhile was going through the laborious process of a Slovenian climbing apprenticeship. There were no shortcuts. You learned to walk – literally – before you could climb, following a curriculum laid down over generations. It was another world of rules. Humar was tutored by one of the old guard, Bojan Pollak, who had been on some of Yugoslavia's biggest successes in the 1970s. He learned to rock climb in heavy mountaineering boots, endured bivouacs without a sleeping bag and went without food and water, all at the behest of his mentor. For Pollak, it was a duty to put something back into the sport. 'Being an alpinist in those days had status,' Prezelj says. 'It was socially more acceptable, not less. You were doing something for the nation. Those who were good at it got the benefits, free holidays and so forth. You were supported by society.'

The beneficiaries of that system felt obliged to put something back. 'Without the help of the state nobody could have gone anywhere,' says Viki Grošelj. 'Our salaries at that time were around $150 a month. An air ticket to Nepal was around $1,000.' Not surprisingly, competition for places on expeditions was intense. The expeditions commission would choose the targets and alpinists would apply to join, attaching their climbing resumes. Prezelj says you had to prove yourself, to show your skill in the mountains to your peers, rather than fluff up your image on your website. 'You couldn't fake it.'

With this system, through the 1970s and 1980s, Slovenian mountaineers notched up a string of hugely impressive first ascents, on Makalu in 1975, Gasherbrum in 1977, Everest in 1979, and Dhaulagiri in 1981. That year another Slovenian expedition made a strong attempt on the south face of Lhotse. Tone Škarja had a plan to put a Slovenian on the summit of every 8,000-metre peak. It took exactly twenty years to complete the project, and in the process Yugoslavia built up a large cadre of experienced high-altitude climbers, almost exclusively Slovenian.

'It's not easy for young Slovenian climbers,' Grošelj says. 'If you want to be the best here, then you've got to be among the best in the world. In 1975, I got on to a national team for the expedition to Makalu's south face. That was after doing twenty-five climbs in 1974, of which ten were relatively good. And for that expedition I was one of the best. Now, if I wish to get national attention, with twenty-five climbs, people would just smile and say come back when you've done a hundred difficult ones.'

The Makalu expedition, which made the first ascent of the south face, was an old-style siege trip with the strongest climbers Slovenia could muster: Stane 'Šrauf' Belak, Tomaž Jamnik, Bojan Pollak, Humar's tutor, and Nejc Zaplotnik, among others. 'We tried to do the best we could on the mountain,' says Grošelj, 'mostly because none of us knew when we'd get a chance to go back. It was a big drive for us all.' But as Tone Škarja says, that put the emphasis more on success than style or difficulty. 'If there were two routes available to us, one hard and safe, the other easier but a bit more risky, our boys preferred the easier but more dangerous one – for speed. They would take the risk.'

With such a large cohort of grizzled Himalayan veterans at the disposal of Slovenia's climbing clubs, it's not surprising the next couple of generations came on strong. More than a decade on from Makalu, Marko Prezelj joined Belak and Grošelj and other legends attempting a new route on Shishapangma. Prezelj had read all their books and wondered how he would keep up with them. As it turned out, they had more trouble keeping up with him, even if he lacked their experience. Prezelj was paired with Belak but the older man was sick and Prezelj moved twice as fast. When Šrauf dropped his rucksack, a frustrated Prezelj was forced to descend. The leader of the expedition, Tone Škarja, decided that with a new route in the bag and the mountain climbed, it was time to go home. This was, Prezelj says, the moment he realised that 'being part of a machine was not for me'.

Influenced by Western climbers, and aware that technical standards in the Himalaya were surging ahead, Prezelj was just one of several Slovenian climbers to start branching out on his own, abandoning the PZS juggernaut for alpine style. Česen was another. Slavko Svetičič got support from the PZS, but climbed his hugely impressive new route on the west face of Annapurna alone. Janez Jeglič, Silvo Karo and Franc Knez switched to alpine style on hard new routes in Patagonia, as well as the Himalaya.

This vibrant new community emerged just as 'the machine' ground to a halt. Then, at the start of the 1990s, Yugoslavia imploded in ethnic violence. Slovenia emerged relatively unscathed from its brief war with Slobodan Milošević's Serbian forces. But with the collapse of socialism, mountaineering's security blanket was gone. 'Less and less money came from the state, but we began to find sponsors,' says Viki Grošelj. 'They could see we were doing well.' Škarja says the PZS managed to support a few organised expeditions, but in the early 1990s were forced to look for private sponsors just like everybody else. The number of expeditions leaving Slovenia more than halved.

Then, like Arnold Schwarzenegger's cyborg in *The Terminator*, Slovenia's expeditions commission flickered back into life. And that's how Tomaž Humar got his big break. No one who knew him in his early years claims that Humar was preternaturally talented as a climber. In the Kamnik club, the talent was Marko Prezelj. But Humar's toughness and energy, as well as his charisma, had made a strong impression. Tone Škarja was planning an expedition to Annapurna in the spring of 1995, the last of the 8,000-metre peaks yet unclimbed by a Slovenian. He needed fresh blood to build his team. Škarja's long-time comrade-in-arms Šrauf Belak, now past his best, was planning an old-farts trip to Ganesh V (6,986 metres) the year before and Škarja asked if he'd take along a couple of young hotshots, Tomaž Humar and Gregor Kresal, if the PZS paid their way. It would be a chance to see if they had what it took for Annapurna. Humar finally had what he'd dreamed about: a ticket to the Himalaya.

It still wasn't easy. Tomaž had married his girlfriend Sergeja in 1991 and they now had a young child, Ursa. He was working flat out at various jobs, from working as an electrician, to managing bank security, to painting, just to keep things together at home and still get out climbing. Now he proposed to leave his family for weeks to go off to the Himalaya. At that early stage, Sergeja could deal with Humar's passion for climbing, and she made the necessary sacrifices.

Humar shone on Ganesh. A general feeling that the team had missed its chance was overturned by Humar's irrepressible determination to succeed. Not for the last time, he ignored an instruction from his leader to descend. In the end, it was the old warhorse Šrauf, then fifty-four, and the young dynamo Humar, who reached the summit. Škarja was delighted. 'They only succeeded because Humar was there,' he told me.

If the old man admired Humar's determination, the independent spirit that had prompted Šrauf Belak to scream in frustration also gave Škarja a headache. The point of the Annapurna expedition was to put the brothers Davo and Drejc Karnicar on the summit so they could make the first ski descent and also put up a new route on the north-west face. Humar was along to hump loads and make these ambitions happen. He wasn't considered a likely candidate for a ticket to the summit.

Times, however, had changed. The PZS no longer offered young climbers the blank cheque it had before independence. That weakened individual commitment to the team. Any sponsorship Tomaž found, Škarja told him, was required for the expedition kitty. But that didn't mean his chances for the summit would be upgraded. So Tomaž refused to donate his money. He welcomed the chance to climb with some old hands like Viki Grošelj, by then a twenty-year veteran, and learned valuable lessons from them. But he wasn't about to bury his personal ambition for the good of the team – not entirely. It's not how the world worked any more.

The Karnicars took their chance, and made the first ski descent of Annapurna. Humar carried loads and pushed the route, but was ordered down from Camp 3 so as not to get in their way. He didn't take it well. Determined to give Annapurna one last shot, Humar went back against Škarja's wishes into the face of worsening weather where he and his Sherpa teammate, Arjun, struggled to find the tents at Camp 4 in zero visibility.

Naively, they opted to rest here for a day. The following morning, after two nights at 7,500 metres, the climbers at base camp were anxious. What happened next is disputed. The weather was bad that morning, and Humar said Škarja told him once again to descend. Humar ignored the order, saying he was going to the summit, even though it was midday and the weather was still poor. But that's not how Škarja remembers it.

'I told him it was better if he went down,' Škarja says. 'But I would never stop a man if he wished to go up. I was angry, yes, but because he actually told me he was coming down. The route between Camp 4 and Camp 2 was very dangerous. We were speculating about where he was, figuring he must be at Camp 3. But we heard nothing on the radio. Two hours pass. Three hours. Nothing. Then at 7 p.m. we heard he was on the summit. For eight hours there was no word from him. He told us he was leaving Camp 4 to come down to base camp.'

On the evidence of Annapurna, it was clear Humar's personality and ambition was not suited to the kind of expedition Tone Škarja was used to leading. He wasn't alone in that. Marko Prezelj had clashed with Škarja, and other Slovenian climbers were forging their own path. Humar liked to complain that the establishment had stood in the way of his career, but Prezelj disagrees. 'It was a personal choice,' he says. 'Slavko Svetičič was a good alpinist but he didn't fit in any official frame either. He could still go on expeditions. Tomaž would complain that he was thwarted by the system but it wasn't true. Not at all. Maybe in the old times, he would have been, yes. But by the time we were going to the Himalaya, that was over.'

Despite their differences on Annapurna, Tone Škarja and the PZS stuck with Humar. His next three Himalayan expeditions all had some kind of official support, and for many of his fellow Slovenian climbers these were his golden years. In 1996, he and his partner Vanja Furlan won a Piolet d'Or for their pre-monsoon ascent of the north-west face of Ama Dablam in a five-day push of backs-to-the-wall alpine climbing that was a league or two above anything Humar had done before in the Himalaya. Tone Škarja's expeditions commission paid for the whole thing.

That autumn he soloed the first ascent of a peak in western Nepal called Bobaye, as part of an all-star team that included Marko Prezelj and another presiding genius of Slovenian mountain climbing, Andrej Stremfelj. A year later, he was back in Nepal for the fifth time in three years, climbing a tough new route on the south face of Nuptse with Janez 'Johan' Jeglič in a five-day push. Steep, risky and an elegant line on a beautiful face, Nuptse showed just how far Humar had come in a short period of time.

This intense burst of activity brought Humar to international attention. Before the Piolets d'Or, few outside the small world of Slovenian climbing had heard of him. After Ama Dablam and Nuptse, people wondered what this extrovert character would do next. Like Reinhold Messner, Viki Grošelj says, Humar developed the knack of taking his career to a new level that captured people's imagination. But while the Italian can seem austere and arrogant, Humar knew how to connect with ordinary Slovenians with no prior interest in his sport.

Moon-faced and with small, paw-like hands, Humar wasn't a wiry athlete who kept himself finely tuned, more a compact bear of a man. His weight fluctuated, and he would rub his belly appreciatively, adding that this was what kept him going when the going got harsh. He would talk seriously and quietly, but then the energy inside him would spill out, and he'd grin and laugh, and his eyes would burst into flame. His broad grin drew people to him. 'Before Tomaž,' Grošelj says, 'I had to explain to my sponsors what alpinism was. After Tomaž, it was no problem. He made climbing big in Slovenia for his enemies, as well as for himself.'

But while Humar found success in the mid 1990s, creating a buzz with his meteoric rise, the seeds of his failure were also sown, some by his own hand, some by fate. First, there was the loss of friends. Šrauf Belak, his mentor on Ganesh, died, alongside his girlfriend, in an avalanche in Slovenia's Julian Alps on Christmas Eve 1995. Vanja Furlan, his partner on Ama Dablam, died in a fall, also in the Julian Alps, the following summer. On Nuptse, Humar's partner Johan Jeglič was blown from the summit in a gathering storm, leaving him to make a harrowing descent alone.

Nuptse had been Jeglič's idea. Coming back from Everest years before, he had spotted a stunning, tenuous line up the peak's impressive south face. Jeglič was undoubtedly a more technically capable climber than Humar. He did it all – big walls in Yosemite and new routes in Patagonia, 8b sport climbs, ice climbing competitions, modern test-pieces in the Alps, even a new variation on Everest. His new route on Bhagirathi III in Garhwal Himal, done with Silvo Karo, impressed most of all. But the weather that autumn was dreadful. As October wore on, teams started packing up and leaving. Humar and Jeglič dug in at a base camp. Well acclimatised after climbing Pumori, they waited a week, and then started climbing on 27 October. Carrying only some five-millimetre Kevlar static line, they sprinted up an ice couloir up to eighty degrees, menaced by séracs, to a ledge at 5,900 metres and their first bivouac. In the morning the weather was grim. In thick cloud and threatened by avalanches, Jeglič and Humar made only another 400 metres and camped in a crevasse, their tent pummelled by a strengthening wind.

Visibility improved on 29 October, but they only climbed another 400 metres of steep mixed ground, strafed by loose rock and ice. They chopped out a ledge and fixed their tent with ice screws, but it was soon buried with snow. Humar woke with a splitting headache as air in the tent grew stale. It was time to dump the bivouac gear and race the last thousand metres to the top. They were moving by 4 a.m. and made good progress, despite a menacing wind. Climbing in their own private bubble, the two men said little, meeting to share a little liquid, joking it was held in their pee bottle. 'We'll rinse it out Johan. It can't hurt. As long as it's liquid.' At 7,500 metres, Jeglič could see the summit of Everest, capped by a frightening lenticular cloud. The ridge above them was howling in the face of a gale. They agreed to keep going until 2 p.m.

Jeglič drew ahead, and at 1 p.m. Humar looked up to see him waving, apparently on the summit. But when Humar arrived fifteen minutes later, there was no sign of him. Jeglič was gone, blasted into oblivion by the savage wind. Humar was utterly alone, stranded on the summit of Nuptse. His descent was a nightmare, spent on the brink of exhaustion. He made their bivouac tent at midnight, and promptly set it on fire after the stove malfunctioned. Base camp stayed on the radio, urging Tomaž to focus, but by the next evening he was hallucinating wildly, and suffering frostbite. It was three days since he'd drunk anything. He was found at the bottom of the face at midnight, marooned in a crevasse field, and led to safety. Coming down from Nuptse, said Humar, was the 'hardest situation in my life. Freezing hell. No water, no nothing.'

The physical wounds – he suffered frostbite in four toes – took months to heal. The psychological scars stayed with him for good. Jeglič was well loved in the Slovenian climbing community, quieter than Humar, less entranced by his own story. And for many, including Viki Grošelj, 'Janez was the better climber at that time. Tomaž was the second.' And even Humar agreed, saying that, 'Jeglič was simply the best. The only mistake he made was his last trip to Nepal.' Despite years of success with partners, after Nuptse, Humar preferred to climb alone. 'When Janez died he left children and this is not easy,' he said. 'I didn't want to come home with [just my partner's] passport and wallet again.'

Grief at his loss prompted some wild accusations about what *really* happened on Nuptse. All this speculation left Humar to comment that the wrong man had come back from the mountain. 'Humar was a lightning conductor for all the different tensions in Slovenian climbing,' says Grošelj. 'He was very sure he was right and wouldn't listen. He couldn't get a perspective on things.' His injuries meant he had nothing to do but brood, revealing a darker aspect of his personality very different from the ebullient enthusiasm he showed his fans. His marriage too was starting to unravel. Sergeja had given birth to their second child, also Tomaž, while his father was on Ama Dablam. The long months of separation and anxiety had taken their toll. When he was gone, she lived with the fear he might not come back. When he did come back, the force of his personality seemed to take over her life. Leafing through the family's photo albums, biographer Bernadette McDonald could see the strain of Humar's obsession etched on Sergeja's face. 'In the early photographs she looks happy, and then as I turned the pages I could see the lines of desperation growing deeper.'

In a magazine profile, writer Peter Maass explained that 'being with Tomaž is not unlike hanging out with a hyperactive child'. Humar, Maass said, would not stop talking. 'He talks about his father, Kamnik, George Bush, environmentalism, abortion, Dhaulagiri, meditation, war, food, wine, Yosemite, hang-gliding, paragliding, Slobodan Milošević, country music, the Internet, pitons, and prosciutto. If we are in the car and I happen to fall asleep, he nudges me awake to tell me more.'

'He must have been hard to live with,' says Viki Grošelj. 'We'd go round there and he'd be incredibly entertaining, but then we'd get to go home and rest.' Sergeja had always been profoundly religious, but her frustration at living with Tomaž pushed her toward a deeper obsession with her faith. She told Maass she chose Tomaž as 'Jesus chose the cross'. But she was clearly anxious about where they were heading and longed for him to take his foot off the gas.

Humar too, talked often about his own spiritual life, which conflated his childhood Catholicism with pretty much every brand of soul food on the market. 'I was born a Christian,' he said, 'but if you believe in Allah or Buddha, the main thing is love. It is all the same.' Buddh-ish just about captures it. He carried a photograph of the Indian spiritual leader Sai Baba, who has faced allegations of fraud and sexual abuse, but whose eclectic attitude to religion suited Humar. He began talking about having a spiritual relationship with mountains, as being living entities.

'The face of the mountain has a soul,' he said. 'Mountains are not dead. They are very living things.' Hallucinations prompted by exhaustion on Nuptse were a spiritual experience that allowed him to survive. He began to think of this as seeing with his third, inner, eye, or what Buddhists would call our inner gate to a higher consciousness. 'When you accept danger, then it is easier to handle,' he said. 'You must understand when you feel the mountain. My third eye [guides me]. Even when you are on loose rock you know which ones will hold.'

Even his friends were sceptical. 'Tomaž reached the limit of where training and experience would take him,' Grošelj says. 'He saw that there was nowhere to improve and maybe he thought his third-eye approach was a way to be better, that if you understand these things you can be a better climber. It was a way of seeing. It wasn't classically religious, not what they say in our churches. And I was different than him in this. I thought it was dangerous, this spiritual thing. We laughed about it. When he came down from Nanga Parbat, I asked him: "Where's your third eye now?" And he laughed. "I don't know. Maybe I dropped it?" It's amazing. People loved him for that stuff. It was a little bit mystical. His arms would wave and people would watch him.'

Driven on by his own momentum, Humar found himself increasingly isolated from the Slovenian climbing establishment. That process reached its climax on Dhaulagiri, the mountain that transformed his life. In his autobiography, *No Impossible Ways*, Humar suggests that his rupture from the PZS occurred during the furious arguments he had with Tone Škarja on Annapurna. Škarja doesn't see it like that. 'Here, at Dhaulagiri, we divide,' he says. The reason wasn't spirituality or the death of friends; it was money, pure and simple. 'He came to us in June or July in 1999. I knew he'd already been to our sponsors on Annapurna asking them why they were giving money to such big expeditions [like ours] when he could do it alone for less. He wanted $10,000, but we were in the red. I told him it was a big risk.'

The phrase 'big risk' is an understatement. The south face of Dhaulagiri is vast, 4,000 metres high and bristling with objective danger. What Humar proposed was like going over the top in World War I. His boyhood mentor Bojan Pollak put the odds of Humar's survival at fifty-fifty. Tomaž himself, after the event, nonchalantly suggested he had a twenty per cent chance of survival. Later he justified the risk. 'In alpinism you need risk. Without risk you don't have alpinism.'

Messner had tried the climb – and failed. A big Polish team had climbed an easier line on the face's left. A Slovenian team had climbed to the right, and then veered on to the east ridge. The true line, the centre of the face, stood untouched, waiting for someone with just the right kind of extreme personality and wild energy to come along and give it a try. Humar fitted the bill perfectly.

When Škarja pulled the rug from under Humar's request for cash, he was infuriated. Humar went into overdrive, phoning contacts and following leads until he got twenty minutes with the Slovenian telecommunications company Mobitel. They agreed to back him and the trip was back on. But in signing up with a large corporate sponsor, Humar broke the mould for Slovenian climbing. He entered a new game, one of managing huge financial and public expectations, which tested his mental strength as much as séracs and stonefall. A lot was riding on Humar's plans, much of it wasn't in his control. He was consulting astrologers to choose the best date to begin climbing, while signing deals with companies that were transforming Slovenia from socialism to the free market. Škarja could only stand aside and admire his former protégé's business acumen.

Humar might have been climbing alone, but he took with him a caravan of friends and helpers to take the edge off the isolation of camping below Dhaulagiri. He also had thousands of armchair mountaineers logging on to follow each twist and turn. This interest in him buoyed Humar, like hot air swells a balloon. The weather in Nepal that autumn was dire. The day before he started, the British mountaineer Ginette Harrison died on the mountain. As Humar set off, a huge avalanche swept down the middle of the face.

Shouldering a heavy pack, he made slow progress on the first day, struck by loose ice and soaked by wet snow and water running down the face. On technical sections he tied off his sack and ran out a five-millimetre Kevlar line that he would abseil down to collect his gear. He carried a few cams, four ice screws and half a dozen pitons. He also carried one of his son's little shoes for good luck. How he felt about the mountain, and how the mountain felt about him, seemed as important as his planning. 'You need to feel and smell like a horse so you are with the mountain,' he said. 'Normally, I don't go on a wall unless I have permission from the wall.'

Despite Humar's gnomic eloquence, Grošelj says it's a mistake to think that he didn't pay attention to detail. 'He was impulsive, yes, but when it came to climbing he was thorough and prepared very well. Stipe told me how unbelievably safe he was. He was precise about things.' Humar would say that training and being prepared were only part of what you needed to stay safe. 'You need to be like a Swiss watch,' he said about his climbing philosophy, but 'also blessed from God and have a lot of luck. Luck is a gift; it is not an absolute. You should be prepared for luck. Luck likes being prepared.'

As the days passed and Humar's little envelope of dreams floated up the face, more and more people back home logged on to check on his progress.

This meant something to him. He drew strength from the impact he was having. He also found he could disassociate his mind from his body's hardships. Battered by falling ice, exhausted after days on the face with little sleep or food, his spiritual focus really did keep him going. At 6,300 metres, he developed a raging toothache, so took his penknife to the filling, releasing the infection beneath and easing the pressure in his head. The audience back home winced in sympathy.

By now, more than two thirds of the way up the south face, Humar realised that if he stuck to his direct line, he wasn't going to make it. And that meant he would die. There was no way off this face, other than up. So he made the decision to follow a line traversing up toward the east ridge, first done by a Japanese team in 1978, and climb the last eight or nine hundred metres to the summit that way. As it turned out, by the ninth day, Humar was so strung out from his last bivouac at 8,000 metres, the game was up. He looked carefully at the pictures of his kids he carried, and headed down, a hundred metres or so below the summit. 'My children trust me,' he would later say, 'father always comes back.' Dhaulagiri, it seemed, would let him have the face, but not the summit.

He arrived home to a tumultuous welcome. His website had received 1.7 million hits a day as the climb reached its climax, and Slovenia was agog to find out more about this voyager on the edge of life. His sponsor Mobitel sent the executive jet to Brussels to collect Reinhold Messner, then a member of the European Parliament, who was waiting in arrivals to endorse Humar's achievement. ('What is he?' one Slovenian climber asked me. 'The climbing pope?')

Messner had one stipulation. No one should mention his earlier acknowledgement of Tomo Česen. 'At the moment,' Messner pontificated, 'Humar is the greatest high-altitude climber in the world. What he has done is special. I know these walls, and they are very difficult, especially Dhaulagiri.' The American alpinist Mark Twight was more insightful: 'The great evolutionary steps in climbing take place because of people expanding their psychological capacity. We can improve our gear and our training, but it doesn't matter unless you can see with enough clarity what is possible. The rest of us just aren't seeing what [Humar] is.'

Closer to home, the flak was soon bursting around Humar's ears. Slovenian critics pointed out that he hadn't reached the summit. Nor had he climbed the true line he'd intended, taking in the whole face, whatever the press were saying. The route was overgraded and overhyped. Humar was little more than a reckless stunt-monkey prepared to accept odds most climbers would think insane.

Ten years on, judgement on Humar's most famous adventure is more nuanced. Marko Prezelj told me: 'Dhaulagiri was a good epic, a good climb, but for me personally it was not a milestone in the development of climbing. Compare it to Slavko Svetičič soloing Annapurna's west face by a new route, technically speaking more difficult, which joined the normal route at 7,900 metres. In 1991. Nobody's ever heard of this though.' Viki Grošelj is more generous. 'He had the balls to start in the middle of that face and he had a plan.' For that, Grošelj suggests, Humar deserves his place in the pantheon. 'In my opinion, Humar's Dhaulagiri climb was the best thing any human had done in the Himalaya.'

A year to the day after his decision to traverse off the south face of Dhaulagiri, Tomaž Humar lay in a broken heap, not at the bottom of a cliff but in what would be the cellar of the new home he was building for Sergeja and their children in the Kamnik Alps. When he regained consciousness, Humar felt something strange weighing down on his body. It was his right leg. He had a broken femur. His left heel was shattered. Humar lost three litres of blood and suffered a pulmonary embolism, flatlining during six-hour emergency surgery. The irony was cruel. Fêted at film festivals and lectures around the world, decorated by the president of Slovenia, hailed on the street by strangers, financially in great shape, it seemed as though the gamble he'd made with fate had paid off. Now he was reduced to a wheelchair. It looked like nemesis had finally caught up with Tomaž Humar.

But it hadn't. Not yet anyway. He was indefatigable in recovery. When the doctors told him not to expect too much, he just laughed. But complications and infection slowed his progress. If he hadn't gone to Germany for further treatment, Humar would have stayed in the wheelchair he dubbed the red Ferrari. Humar said he recovered 'with the help of God. No medicine.' He subjected himself to unorthodox cures. He meditated, getting his heart rate up to 200 beats per minute, then immersed himself in cold water. This, he said, 'tempers the body'. The recovery took two years.

Looking back, several of those close to Humar agree that he was not the same force after the accident. But, what he did soon after was impressive enough, considering the severity of his injuries that left him '30.5 per cent crippled'. He climbed Shishapangma with a Kazakh team as part of his rehabilitation, and a new route on Aconcagua's south face with a young lad from the Kamnik club, Ales Kozelj, earned him a third nomination for the Piolets d'Or. Humar's route on Aconcagua, he said, was the most difficult; 'not even one ice screw or piton' for protection. That climb, he said, was under one big sérac. 'A one-way ticket; I like one-way tickets.'

Constantly, it seemed, he was locked in some kind of mystical internal struggle. In 2004, five years since his last significant success, Humar said that he needed to get back to hard climbing to 'compete with my weakness', noting that he had 'black holes' in his aura. 'You have to follow the way,' he said, 'and He will take care of you.' In 2005, he was back in Nepal climbing Cholatse with Kozelj and Janko Oprešnik, from the Annapurna expedition. While they were on the mountain, Ueli Steck, a star from the next generation, still in his twenties, was soloing a new variant in thirty-seven hours. At times, he must have felt his future was behind him.

Nanga Parbat would give Tomaž his second chance. A new route, climbed alone, up the Rupal face would outdo even his Dhaulagiri success. He arrived in Pakistan in the summer of 2005, once again with the backing of Mobitel and the eyes of the world on him. On his website he spelled out just how committing his climb would be. 'If it was easy to get rescued, someone would have tried to climb this route before. All mountaineers who decide to do such a feat know there might be no way back.' Those words would return to haunt him.

Humar was not in the right frame of mind for such a gigantic undertaking. His marriage to Sergeja had collapsed and his thoughts were not exclusively on the mountain. 'Messner once said you must be calm, in balance with yourself, before you make an extreme climb,' says Viki Grošelj. 'But Tomaž in the last few years had a big problem with this.'

Soon after he started up the face, Humar became stranded, trapped in a small hole in the ice at over 6,000 metres, threatened on all sides by avalanches. He couldn't go up or descend. His desperate position was broadcast around the world, as international efforts got under way to rescue him. It took the personal intervention of the Pakistani president General Pervez Musharraf to allow an unprecedented helicopter rescue, and the extraordinary skill of Pakistani air force pilot Rashid Ullah Baig to pull it off. Humar had been marooned for ten days, and was close to the end. Slovenian television devoted twenty minutes to his lucky escape. He was photographed back at base camp, kneeling on the ground, his head pressed against the earth in gratitude. Humar returned home, calling his rescue a second birth, to the relief of his fans and the vitriol of his critics.

After Nanga Parbat, everything changed. He withdrew, literally and psychologically. Tomaž Humar's second life was lived far from the attention of the media. Viki Grošelj had spoken to him via satellite phone during the rescue, and was struck by the change Nanga Parbat made in him. 'He was happy to be alive,' he says. 'But being rescued wasn't good for his ego. Reinhold said the same. He met him in Pakistan at the time.

Tomaž came down very euphoric but he didn't come back to his own life. At that time he started to close himself off.'

If Dhaulagiri had made Tomaž Humar a star, then the expectations for his attempt on Nanga Parbat were colossal. His failure was dramatic and horribly public. His philosophical musings now rang hollow. After such a public rescue, involving risk to others, having your own biotherapist on hand to read the mountain's aura made him seem not so much colourful as bonkers. More hurtful were the brickbats tossed in by other alpinists. Mark Twight was aghast at what had turned into a circus: 'Now every ill-prepared sad sack whose ability falls short of his Himalayan ambition can get on the radio, call for help, and expect the cavalry to save the day.'

The failure hit Humar hard. When he did emerge – to climb on Annapurna's south face, or attempt a last-ditch rescue for compatriot Pavle Kozjek lost on Muztagh Tower – interest in the fading star was mixed with jeers. Only those closest to him knew how sensitive he was. In public, Bernadette McDonald says, he could seem brash and only concerned about his own ambitions. 'My impression, however, was that he was an emotionally fragile person, and those things hurt him a lot, the kind of things people were saying. That he should have been a man and died up there.'

In the autumn of 2009, the Italian alpinist Simone Moro found himself unexpectedly in Kathmandu. He'd been acclimatising in Nepal, before going to Cho Oyu inside Tibet, but the Chinese authorities suddenly revoked his team's visas and permit on political grounds. It was the six-tieth anniversary of the People's Republic, and they weren't taking any chances. One morning, Moro ran into an old friend walking down the street – Tomaž Humar. The two had dinner together, and Humar showed Moro an old photocopied image of Langtang Lirung's south face.

'Tomaž said the face had been attempted two or three times before and that everybody failed,' Moro told me. He agreed to give Humar some ice screws, made by their shared sponsor, CAMP. 'The line he showed me looked to be the only one possible on that face, with less risk than other lines. But it still looked quite dangerous. Tomaž told me also that alpinism had become for him a hobby and no more his job or main activity. He was different from the other times I met him. He also phoned me while he was going by bus to the last village where he intended to start trekking.' It was, Moro thinks, a final greeting.

Apart from Moro, almost no one knew that Humar was in Nepal. Certainly not anyone at the PZS, or even Viki Grošelj who had, he says, tried to keep his relationship with Humar on an even keel. Separated and then divorced from Sergeja several years before, Humar had fought a long battle to maintain contact with his children. When Humar died, Sergeja didn't attend the funeral, or allow the children to go. A long relationship with Slovenian journalist Maja Ros, begun on Nanga Parbat, broke down in 2008. His business, running a rope-access company, allowed him a decent enough living, thanks to a government contract. But Grošelj adds that he wasn't as well off as he had been or as many of his critics believed him to be.

What was in Tomaž Humar's mind as he left base camp for the last time? At 3,300 metres, the south face of Langtang Lirung is one of the biggest in the Himalaya, and its reputation is sobering. Mike Searle, leader of the British attempt on Langtang's south-west face in 1980, recalled avalanches down the face taking four minutes to reach the bottom. In 2015, during a devastating earthquake, an avalanche triggered on this face destroyed Langtang village. More than 300 people died. Searle's group had started from Langtang village, down the valley from Kyanjin Gompa at 3,500 metres. It took them weeks of effort to climb thousands of metres up a steep wall and talus to the midway point, a huge bowl in the centre of the face. Then they ran out of steam.

Humar hit on an alternative approach that gave his bold solo attempt a real chance. At the end of the first week in November, he left base camp on the Langtang Glacier and climbed up to the col on the south ridge. Here, on 8 November, he called Jagat, his friend and base camp manager. What happened next isn't clear. Either he traversed, or more likely abseiled, down to easier ground at the foot of the col and then traversed into the heart of the south-west face. Mike Searle recalls that, 'none of us were particularly keen to dodge the avalanches on the ice slopes above'. The route was climbable, he says, 'but the objective dangers were too great'. It's easy to imagine Humar being struck by ice or rock, and falling the next day, 9 November.

Nobody I spoke to was surprised that Tomaž Humar died this way. 'Hopefully, I'll have a long life,' he said before Nanga Parbat. 'But I probably won't see fifty. I don't think much about retirement.' Dead at forty, Humar didn't get close to even his pessimistic prediction.

Bernadette McDonald last saw him a year before his death at a film festival in Scotland. 'He wasn't well. He had some kind of lead poisoning and was seeing a doctor in Germany. He was goofing around like he always did in public, but in private he was worried.' McDonald speculates that his years painting as a young man, raising cash for expeditions, may have come back to haunt him. His poor health was undermining future climbing plans. 'He seemed to me a smaller version of his former self,' she adds.

He had, however, started a new relationship and it was his girlfriend who alerted Grošelj to Humar's predicament. He had called her, and not Jagat, after being badly injured on 9 November. She asked if he could help organise a rescue. Grošelj contacted Gerold Biner, who had overseen the Pakistani rescue, and since Biner was recovering from surgery, he put the task in the hands of Bruno Jelk. He also contacted Humar's Nepali agent, Ang Tshering. On Wednesday 10 November, Humar called Jagat. 'I have broken my back and leg,' he said. 'I am afraid it will be difficult for a helicopter to locate me. My pulse is weak and I think I am going to die. This is my last … '

Ang Tshering was already organising a flight by Fishtail to Langtang to drop a search team. They reached the south ridge from where Humar had called Jagat on 8 November, the next morning, but could see no sign of him. Bad weather on Thursday and Friday, when the Swiss arrived in Kathmandu, prevented any further search.

How Tomaž Humar spent his final days is a mystery that may never be explained. But among the speculation are some clues. Anthamatten wondered what his climbing plans were. Why cross the south ridge and go down? Humar had studied the face and previous attempts. Perhaps, by coming in from the other side of the south ridge and dropping down to the glacier above this section, Humar thought he could save himself over 1,500 metres of hard climbing – an ingenious solution to the problem that had bogged down the British in 1980.

Why did he call his girlfriend first, a day before calling his base camp manager? Grošelj says Tomaž didn't ask her to get help. Uttterly alone and expecting to die, he just wanted some human contact. Did he really not want a rescue effort made? It seems unlikely. A lodge owner in Kyanjin Gompa told British trekkers he had Humar's sat phone number and called him. Humar, the lodge owner said, was desperate for help to come. He wanted to live. Could more have been done to rescue him? Close friends feel if the Swiss had been called sooner, then perhaps he might have survived. But Humar was vague about his plans, and climbing in a totally committed style. No one knew better the consequences of an accident – and how unlikely a rescue might be – than Humar himself. Finally, where was his gear? His sleeping bag and stove? Viki Grošelj speculates that he fell from a bivouac site where his gear was stashed.

On his last climb, Tomaž Humar turned his back on the media. He seemed driven only by an inner compulsion to climb what he excelled at – a big, serious, Himalayan face. Whether he was looking for redemption, or a return to the limelight, at some level Langtang Lirung was the kind of stage where he could most fully act out his life's dramas. Yet even in death, Humar still divides opinion like almost no one else.

'It was a shock,' says Tone Škarja, without appearing at all shocked. 'He was a national hero. For non-climbers he was the greatest climber in Slovenia. But time moves on. The public forgets.' Škarja is already looking to the next generation of Slovenian masters. 'The direction of Marko Prezelj is the best way – safe and technical climbing.' Prezelj was in the Garhwal Himal last year, climbing with two young hotshots, Rok Blagus and Luka Lindič. 'This was excellent,' Škarja says.

Journalists often ask him if Tomaž Humar was Slovenia's most influential climber, but he tells them no. The name he offers is that of Nejc Zaplotnik, who reached the summit of Everest in 1979 via the west ridge, wrote a book called *The Way*, then died in an avalanche on Manaslu in 1983. 'Zaplotnik really opened new horizons for young climbers. Tomaž's life was very different from the way he told it. Tomaž became rich, much more that any other climber. Everything Zaplotnik did was for alpinism.'

Bernadette McDonald is more forgiving. 'When I was writing my book, I had the sense that Tomaž was a kind of tragic character, not just in the life and death sense, but in his everyday life. He was so conflicted about everything and it kind of tore at him. When I talked with him about it, he laughed that I could be so misguided about his character. But I think I was right.'

Big Guts

2011

There's a story the British star Jerry Moffatt tells about a trip he made with Kurt Albert to the bouldering paradise of Hampi in the Indian state of Karnataka. This was in the early 1990s, when few climbers had been there, and the massive plateau sprinkled with golden granite boulders was still being explored. One morning he and Kurt crossed the Tungabhadra River in the little pitch-covered wicker coracle that served as a ferry and found a beautifully shaped block with a steep wall. As often happens in India, a crowd quickly gathered to watch as Albert tried to muscle his way up, only to drop to the ground.

Kurt Albert was a Bavarian oak, six foot one inch, twelve and a half stone, naturally powerful, with thick arms and broad shoulders. At this point in his life, he was well into the second phase of his exceptional climbing career. In the first phase he brought free climbing to West Germany, where he set new standards and developed a new way of climbing. He even gave it a name: redpointing.

When he could no longer keep pace with the revolution he'd launched, he reinvented himself as a new kind of free climber on big walls from Pakistan to Patagonia, joining Germany's best climbers to make the first free ascent of the *Yugoslav Route* (VI, 7a+) on Nameless Tower, and the first ascent of *Royal Flush* (7c, A2), on the east pillar of Fitz Roy. In the early 1990s, Albert began a series of expeditions employing a new twist on the alpine ideal of 'fair means', renouncing motorised support or porters while climbing massive routes like *Fitzcarraldo* (VIII+, 5.12b) in the Cirque of the Unclimbables. For this challenge he and his partners walked and canoed 1,200 miles to approach and return. By the time he went to Hampi with Jerry Moffatt, the transformation – from honed, calorie-counting sport climber to freewheeling caballero – was complete.

One of the Indian onlookers, a slight figure dressed in flimsy cotton, walked over and looked up at this titan with his shaggy hair and thick moustache, pumped up and breathing hard, like Thor at the end of a workout. The Indian's thin brown hands reached up to Albert's swollen biceps and gave them a firm squeeze. Then he looked into the German's face, and said: 'Very big guts.'

In September 2010, Kurt Albert, now fifty-six years old, was guiding a group of novices, a crew of friends from the same soccer team, on a *via ferrata* in the Frankenjura region north of his home town of Nuremberg at a landmark called Höhenglücksteig. It translates as: 'the path where you feel glad to be high up'. Kurt had driven through the night, returning from a slide show in Hamburg. Managing on an hour's sleep, he was standing on a wide ledge, leaned back into his harness, perhaps to rest, perhaps for a clearer view of something, and then he was gone. A karabiner was left on the safety wire; the sling into his harness was empty. He landed head first on a boulder.

When the life-support machine was finally switched off, the German media hailed a fallen hero. Albert had been awarded the highest sporting accolade in Germany, the *Silberne Lorbeerblatt*, a man who had transformed his sport and kept the crowds laughing with his slapstick humour. Yet despite the warm eulogies, beyond the initial sense of loss and shock, the gap Albert has left behind still seems vast. It feels like there's more to be said. Behind the stories of wild times and great deeds, there was something else about Kurt. Something exemplary.

A week or so after Kurt's memorial service I was drinking coffee with Norbert Sandner at his home just outside Nuremberg, a prosperous city that is stolidly Bavarian and just a teensy bit dull. Sandner had known Albert as long as anybody. They shared an apartment and many adventures when they were young, and when Norbert had children and became more settled, he acted as an anchor for Kurt to tie himself to when he needed a mooring.

Sandner handed me a fresh cup of the good stuff while he explained how one of Albert's favourite tricks worked. This one involved apparently hurling a full cup of coffee at someone while all the while hanging on to it, essentially to scare the bejesus out of the victim. Another favourite ruse was secretly slotting a beer mat under a tablecloth and then propping a glass of beer against it at an angle, giving the impression that he had a preternatural sense of balance.

From time to time, a trick would go wrong and no one would laugh harder than Kurt himself. Norbert recalled him losing his grip on a coffee cup and showering someone in cappuccino. Jerry Moffatt was enjoying an après-ski drink with Albert in the late 1980s, when he tried the balancing trick to impress some girls, and sent a full glass of *weissbier* everywhere. At his memorial service, as his friends packed away the champagne glasses, Moffatt suggested they smash one because, as everyone agreed, Kurt would have.

Some of Albert's gags were shockingly hard-core, but only at his own risk. Take, for instance, the time he blew his Achilles tendon tower jumping in what was then Czechoslovakia. Tower jumping is one of those age-old cultural traditions boys perform to impress girls (or each other) after a beer or two – the Czech equivalent of running with the bulls in Pamplona. One notoriously awkward, roped leap required Kurt to catch a big flake on the opposite wall. Miss it, and he'd swing back into the launching tower and smack his head. People had died doing just that.

Kurt thought about it. He had, after all, trained as a high-school physics teacher. He understood angles, velocity and distance: all the stuff that's critical in sticking a tower jump. And it was doubly important to get it right, because he was doing it on German television. He patiently explained to the camera how he had paid out more slack than necessary, so if he fell, he would swing harmlessly below the undercut wall.

'Nothing can happen,' he concluded to camera.

Kurt leaped, missed the hold, and in a moment replete with all the grim humour the gods usually reserve for jackasses, the loop of slack hooked around his ankle and then tightened violently as his weight came on the rope. Kurt's Achilles tendon went pop and he was lowered to the ground. The crew rushed to his side but he held up his hands – 'No, it's okay!' – and hopped back to his car.

'Typical Kurt,' says Moffatt, who found himself a few years later standing on top of the same tower, this time for a British television show, interviewing Kurt about the accident. 'The only way I'm jumping off this tower again is if someone pushes me off,' Albert said to the camera, at which point Moffatt slammed him in the chest and sent him over the edge for a thirty-footer. 'The whole thing was Kurt's idea,' Moffatt said, then, adopting a mock German accent: 'Hup! It will be funny.'

The stories pile up on each other. Like the time Albert was filmed climbing an overhang built across the roof of an indoor hall. Kurt dropped on to the last, *very* distant bolt and took a huge but carefully calculated pendulum – straight into the cameraman.

The clowning gone wrong became part of his shtick during slideshows. 'Even in the Frankenjura,' says Sandner, 'where everyone had seen his shows, he'd draw an audience of 500 because he was so funny and entertaining. It wasn't like an Alex Huber show that's technically perfect. There'd be mistakes, slides on the floor, that kind of thing. The Huber brothers are pros, and act like it. Kurt would never say he was a professional.'

Kurt Albert's greatest achievement, then, was to pull off a spellbinding balancing act. He embraced climbing's absurdity, while simultaneously revelling in its grandeur. He was a joker, yet capable of intense effort and concentration, especially with friends who were equally enthusiastic. His 1989 ascent of the *Eternal Flame* (VI, 7b+, A2 with three points of aid) on Nameless Tower in the Karakoram is a good example. With two partners already home in Germany and Wolfgang Güllich injured, Albert took the lead, persevered and advanced the route to the summit. 'In his heart he was a cowboy,' says the ex-patriot American climber Jesse Guthrie, an erstwhile rodeo competitor himself. 'He loved the Utah deserts. He loved the big open spaces. No rules, no regulations.'

Kurt was born wild. He grew up with his parents and elder brother in an apartment in south Nuremberg. His dad worked as a sales manager for Schöller, which still makes Nuremberg's famous gingerbread, or *Lebkuchen*. Years later, while touring his old neighbourhood with Jerry Moffat, he pointed out the building where he had lived as a child. 'It was four or five floors,' Moffatt recalled. 'Kurt pointed to the guttering where his best mate dared him to traverse across. It was about five metres, from one balcony to the next.' Kurt said he'd shot across it but Moffatt remarked that the traverse looked terrifying for a climber, let alone a small boy.

'Oh, jumping off the top board at the swimming pool was even more scary,' Albert replied. Jerry was surprised and asked why. 'Because I couldn't swim. I had to jump right next to the edge so I could hang on to the side when I came up.'

Then they passed the church his family attended. 'And that's where the priest chased me down the road for mucking around during confession. He shouted at me never to come back.'

Instead, Kurt settled on a church of his own choosing, joining the local section of the Deutscher Alpenverein (DAV), the German Alpine Club. His brother Horst, who is an antiques dealer, climbed too, but as Sandner says, '[Kurt] became so good and so famous so soon, that competing was hard. Kurt was so strong, and muscular from a young age.' By the time he was sixteen, Kurt had done routes like the Walker Spur on the Grandes Jorasses and the *1938 Route* on the Eiger.

'He was a real talent,' says Sandner. 'We were in two different DAV sections and there was a bit of competition. My section thought I was the best, his thought he was the best.' Then they met, and instantly became friends, and Albert moved in. At that time, however, German climbing was off the pace. In the United States and Britain, and soon after in France, a campaign was already underway to rid climbs of their points of aid. But in Germany, the stubby cliffs of the Frankenjura were seen merely as training for the big mountains. 'When we met we were both aid climbers,' Sandner says. 'A bit of free between the pegs, but if it got harder, say 6b or 5.10c, then we'd grab something and try to be fast.' On trips they were doing big alpine rock routes in the Wilder Kaiser or the Wetterstein. On the weekends they'd be hanging from pegs at home.

All that changed for Kurt in 1972 when he went to Elbsandstein, near Dresden, then in East Germany. Sandner had been there first, and can still remember the overwhelming impact it had on him. 'It was so foreign for us. It was much more of a shock than going to the States. Everything was so limited. You needed an invitation; you couldn't drive there, only go by train. You couldn't even bring a newspaper. It was like we were coming from the moon.' The climbing, on the other hand, was superb and totally free. Kurt was staggered to discover routes at F5c (5.10) done in the 1920s.

'Before,' Kurt said in 1993, 'all I was doing was aid, and I could do every route. I realised that free climbing was what I wanted to do.' He and Bernd Arnold, the bold free climber responsible for pioneering so many hard routes on the sandstone towers of the Elbsandstein, became good friends, and he experimented with climbing barefoot. 'Kurt was stronger than Bernd,' Sandner says, 'but he respected him for the serious climbing [he'd done] in the Elbsandstein.'

It took a little while for Kurt to replicate the pure free-climbing ethic he'd witnessed outside Dresden on the crags around his home in Nuremberg, but by 1975 he was freeing as many aid routes as he could, the climbing equivalent of shooting fish in a barrel. And to show other climbers that a route could be done without pulling on pegs or stepping in etriers, he painted a red circle at the base of the climb. 'We had a spray can,' says Sandner, 'that you'd use on cars. At the beginning, the old climbers didn't like it. The red dots were pretty big. The last ones he did with nail varnish and a little brush.'

Albert's tactic was to only paint the dot once he climbed the route clean in one lead, rather than using the yo-yo tactics then standard in the States and Britain. History is a little murky on whether Kurt was the originator of this style. Something similar was going on in France around the same time. But redpointing has become the gold standard free-climbing ethic the world over, and is the term we all use to describe a clean ascent.

The following year, the American climber Henry Barber passed through Frankenjura while taking up an invitation from Bernd Arnold to visit Elbsandstein. Kurt, Norbert and the little band of free climbers springing up in the Frankenjura were blown away. '[Henry] was very influential,' Sandner recalls. 'He only climbed with a swami belt, so we got rid of our chest harnesses and did the same. Then John Bachar came, and he really set the standard here.'

Bachar's legendary obsession with training opened a door in Albert's mind, and he began to train more systematically. 'The Germans had a great respect for the American climbing lifestyle,' says Jesse Guthrie. 'When Bachar came over the first time, those guys were really impressed, even though John was not the typical American climber. But they liked that Camp 4 mentality.'

Albert and Sandner visited Yosemite for the first time in 1977, and Kurt went to the States so often through the 1980s that he kept a truck at Guthrie's house, then in Boulder. 'He was fascinated with John Gill,' Guthrie says. 'He was often at Fort Collins and around the Front Range, doing Gill problems. He was interested in how early Gill was doing his training programs. Kurt was scientific. He did experiments with training.'

By then, Sandner and Albert had rented an apartment in Oberschöl-lenbach, north of Nuremberg. Or rather their girlfriends had. Norbert and Kurt simply went climbing and called home every so often until the place was ready. That apartment on Moselstraße 7, which Albert shared later with Wolfgang Güllich, became one of the most significant addresses in free-climbing history. It was essentially open house for the best sport climbers of the 1980s, people like Ben Moon, Ben Masterson, Ron Fawcett, Christian Griffith, Jesse Guthrie, Ron Kauk and John Bachar. There could be twenty people staying at once, with the overspill sleeping in the bath. People would steal gear and make phone calls abroad without paying, and Albert and Güllich wouldn't flinch. More important, in an era before the Internet, their little kingdom was a hub of ideas and information.

The neighbours would look askance at some of the antics of the ever-changing cast, and once or twice the police were called. Jerry Moffatt even ended up signing posters for one cop whose kid was a fan. It always seemed to work out. But Moffatt, like most who stayed there, still can't get over the generosity. 'If you went to Germany they'd look after you. They were incredibly hospitable. They'd show you new routes. They wanted you to do things that hadn't been done. And these were three-star classics. They wanted you to have a great trip. If you went to France, the climbers there weren't going to say, "Look, I've bolted this line, I've tried it a couple of times, it's going to be a classic, why don't you have a go?" No way.'

When Sandner moved out, Güllich, the promising youngster from the Pfalz region, moved in. Albert's girlfriend, Ingrid Reitenspieß, with whom he had his first serious relationship, became Wolfgang's girlfriend.

Pretty soon Wolfgang took Kurt's position as the leading sport climber in Germany, too. If Albert felt aggrieved, he didn't show it. All three would sit on the sofa in the basement watching television together.

'You never saw him angry or jealous,' Sandner says. 'But when Wolfgang became famous, Kurt gave up a little. He wasn't as motivated as he had been.' Even so, many contemporaries felt that Albert was the more naturally gifted climber. 'Wolfgang wasn't a great on-sighter,' Sandner says. 'On form, I would say Kurt was the better all-round climber, although maybe not as powerful.' Jerry Moffatt agrees: 'Wolfgang could be pretty shaky and dragged his feet. Kurt had more finesse. He wasn't as supple as Stefan [Glowacz] is, but he calculated everything. He'd have it all figured out. He wasn't shaky, just strong and accurate with his feet.'

If anything, Jesse Guthrie says, Albert himself was most impressed by Moffatt. 'Kurt was awestruck by Jerry. He would say quite calmly that Jerry Moffatt was the best climber in the world. Better than Wolfgang. Mostly because Jerry could do stuff so quick and on-sight what nobody else could touch. He had tremendous respect for Jerry.'

On his first trip to Germany, having driven overnight crushed in the back of Güllich's VW Golf, Moffatt went straight out and climbed Albert's masterpiece *Sautanz* (IX-, 7b+), which had been the hardest route in Germany in 1981. The Australian star Kim Carrigan, who had done the fastest ascent so far in just three days, was also staying at Albert and Güllich's and came along to belay. Despite the lack of sleep and long journey, Moffatt fought his way to the top first go. Then he did the same to John Bachar's newer test-piece *Chasin' the Trane* (IX, 7c) and capped that with an on-sight repeat of Güllich's *Heisse Finger* (IX, 7c). Pretty soon he had added his own Frankenjura super route, at a grade harder: *The Face*, the first 8a (X-) in Germany.

There were two responses to Moffatt's blitz. Head for the gym, or do something else. Albert and Güllich headed for the gym. Sandner was a member at a local fitness centre called Campus, and Albert went along to use the pull-up bar he'd installed. Pretty soon the climbers asked to use a quiet, empty corner to build a wooden structure with finger ledges – the very first campus board. 'I see them everywhere now,' Sandner says. 'When I think of how it started, I have to laugh.'

Moffatt recalls them training but was also amazed at how naturally powerful Albert was. 'He could always do one-arm pull-ups. Always. And he was a big bloke. He was heavy. Yet he never got injured. Never hurt a tendon. Never did his elbows. He was just this great big Bavarian brick of muscle.' That didn't stop Albert trying to match Moffatt's starvation diet on a visit to the French sport-climbing Mecca of Buoux, where they ate just 1,500 calories a day. At times Albert was almost too weak to walk to the base of the crag.

His mother, who died shortly before Kurt, would bake him cakes. 'Kurt would sit there and say, "Maybe I could have a little slice," and then eat the whole thing,' Moffatt says.

For those too young to remember, it's hard to explain just how quickly sport climbing changed things. It was like a big bang. Moffatt climbing 8a in 1982 was a huge deal. In less than 10 years, six grades were added to the scale, culminating with Güllich's 9a (XI), *Action Directe*. Things moved on much more quietly for the next twenty years.

Keeping up with that pace of change was always going to be tough and Albert was a little bit older than the new stars emerging. Wolfgang seemed quieter than Kurt, but was much more focused on himself, his career and training. That simply wasn't what Kurt Albert was about. 'Kurt was really smart,' says Sandner. 'He knew he had to live from his slide shows and contracts and he couldn't compete any more with the top German climbers. So he decided to bring those free-climbing impulses to the big mountains.'

In 1987, with Gerald Sprachmann, Kurt did the first free ascent of the *Swiss Route* (IX, 7b+) on the Cima Ovest and followed that up with the first free ascent of the famous *Brandler-Hasse* (VIII+, 7a+) on the Cima Grande, both in the Italian Dolomites. The next year he travelled to the Karakoram of Pakistan with Güllich and Hartmut Münchenbach, freeing the *Yugoslav Route* on the Nameless Tower. From then on, each year brought another big, remote, difficult, free first ascent, from Greenland to Patagonia, from the Dolomites to the tepuis of Venezuela.

The freedom of those now-distant days in Oberschöllenbach could never have lasted, but the end was cruel. Ingrid, Norbert Sandner says, both loved and hated the lifestyle she experienced with Kurt and Wolfgang. A lawyer by day, Ingrid would come home at night to dirtbags from half a dozen countries sleeping on her floor. She moved out and married, but for some reason things – life – just didn't work for her any more. In 1991, her husband, who was a friend of both her former boyfriends, found her in their garage asphyxiated by her car exhaust.

In the summer of 1992, Wolfgang Güllich crashed his BMW driving home from an early radio interview. Like Kurt, his life ended when his respirator was switched off. Like Kurt, there wasn't a mark on his well-trained body. Norbert Sandner was there to see his friend die. He tracked down Albert in Yosemite to give him the news. '[Kurt] decided not to come home. He thought there was nothing to be done. He said, "It's all over."'

Kurt Albert never stopped learning. Perhaps that was the most impressive thing about him. He was open to the world. He became fluent in Spanish after he started dating his Spanish girlfriend, Ari. He learned guitar, and then piano, spending up to five hours a day practising. To prepare for expeditions, he would train with Suzi, the name he gave his jumar, plugging up routes like *Tower of Power* again and again. His mind was as fresh as ever, and if he could feel his body starting to fail, that was just another source of humour.

Careless of convention, he would never reply to a dinner invitation, or send a birthday card, but if you needed money, he would toss you his wallet. 'If you were ever in danger, or things were going wrong,' Moffatt says, 'the man you wanted with you was Kurt.'

Just before I leave, Norbert Sandner takes a call. Kurt's local friends are organising a dinner that evening, for one last goodbye. After Sandner hangs up, he says again he still can't believe Kurt has gone.

'He lived the best life I could imagine. He was able to do what he wanted to do. He controlled his life more than anyone I knew. Every day.'

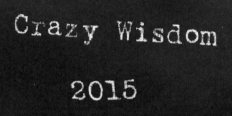

Crazy Wisdom

2015

It had been a grim week in Kathmandu. I'd spent several days tracking events on Everest, talking to those flying back from the mountain in helicopters that carried those killed and injured in the avalanche of 18 April, the worst accident in the mountain's history. After all that, and the drama of another landing at Lukla, I now felt liberated, glad to have stepped back from such intensity, if only for a while as I walked to base camp to report on the tense aftermath.

The cold mountain air tickled my nose. Beside the Dudh Kosi, the milk river, I stopped to watch the morning sunlight filtering through the pines. Luxuriating in the moment, I became aware of someone walking toward me, a young girl, perhaps nine years old, dressed for school, a satchel on her back, singing softly to herself and twirling a flower in her fingers. She paused right in front of me, looked up, as though standing beneath one of those tall pines, and examined my face – one more foreign *kuire* from the thousands who parade through this valley each spring. Then her face creased in a smile, and she slipped the flower into my right hand. I felt her fingers briefly against mine before she walked on, singing to herself again while I uncurled my hand to look at her gift.

Who would not be enchanted? Such innocent impulses of generosity are rare at home. It felt like a blessing, as if I were being shown something, a trusting openness, a warm alternative to the snarky mistrust and resentment that underpins our public discourse. If only our world could be more human and less materialistic, I thought, a place where strangers have time for each other and children trust adults.

These experiences, these moments of revelation, seem to me the sweetest poison. Not because they don't mean something, but because they lead us astray. Like explorers scanning a new-found land, we see something familiar, reach for it – and lose our bearings. Shorn of cultural understanding, ignorant of language, cut loose from history, such simple human gestures leave us exhilarated. We think we've experienced the world as it truly is, but we haven't. We've fooled ourselves. It's made in our heads.

We brought it with us.

This version of the Himalaya is projected through the lens of more than a century of mythmaking. We emerge from a culture that has fed on Rudyard Kipling's *Kim* or James Hilton's *Lost Horizon*. Many of us think Shangri-La is real. This Himalaya is somewhere beyond the everyday, a place of spiritual power immune from our material obsessions. We know that, and we look for it when we come. Charles Snead Houston went through this process more than sixty years ago. With his father Oscar, Andy Bakewell, Betsy Cowles and Bill Tilman, Houston was the first Westerner to visit Khumbu and the Tengboche monastery beyond Namche:

'There we had found a small community, centred in religion, self-sufficient, self-respecting, happy and healthy. Surrounded by scenery beyond description, this small lamasery and attendant village seemed to us a beautiful oasis in a troubled world. In all our travels we met nothing but friendliness and courtesy, and some of the people we met were extraordinarily kind to us. Our eyes were opened to a different way of life, a different religion. It was hard to return from this happy primitive land to a world in which our first news was of the UN reverses in Korea and of political unrest along many borders. It seemed at least debatable that we were returning to civilization.'

Houston's instinct, that we have much to learn from people in the Himalaya, was – is – a good one, but he was sometimes overly sentimental, swept along by the romance, caught up, unconsciously, in older colonialist fantasies of untainted, archaic realms. Tilman was a tougher nut, having turned eighteen fighting at the Somme in 1916. He rarely spoke of the blood and horror. His only real comment on surviving that catastrophe was to quote Coleridge: 'And a thousand thousand slimy things/ Lived on; and so did I.'

Houston imagined for himself a more wholesome way of living; Tilman saw glass in the windows of Namche, paid for with remittances of men escaping grinding poverty and social exclusion to work in the modern town of Darjeeling. He pictured the future: the gimcrack lodges, the herds of half-interested trekkers grazing at souvenir stalls. He knew how the world worked.

Tilman's friend Eric Shipton, more gregarious and rebellious, was thrilled by the who's-better-than-us attitude he found in the Sherpas he hired. On their way to explore the Nanda Devi Sanctuary in 1934, Tilman and Shipton had failed to find their crew of porters at Calcutta's Howrah railway station. What did Sherpas know of trains? Their insouciant arrival left Shipton relieved – and excited:

'Exotic was a mild adjective. Clad in shirts and shorts, and crowned with billycock hats from under which glossy black pig-tails descended, the three were distinctive enough, but when one took into consideration that their shirts were a blinding purple in colour and that this crude shade was matched in their lips and teeth (the result of much betel-chewing) one understood how even the most myopic ticket-collector would notice them … For the next five months we were to live and climb together, and the more we saw of the Sherpas the more we grew to like them. Porters all the time, they were also fellow mountaineers and companions, in turn playing the parts of housekeeper, cook, butler, pantryman, valet, interpreter and, on occasion, entertainer.'

This has been a common Western narrative throughout the long association of Sherpas with mountaineering, a story told over and over again: far from being invisible, Sherpas are ubiquitous – but almost always typecast as a servant class, their characters constructed in ways that reflected the outlook of their employers. To Paul Bauer, leading a Nazi-backed expedition to Nanga Parbat in 1938, they were 'children of nature' too emotionally fragile to witness the frozen victims of the 1934 disaster. (In Heinrich Himmler's surreal mythology, they were also a lost Aryan race.)

In Shipton's writings, they are at least individuals, albeit ones with eccentricities on display, like an Orientalist fantasy of the Admirable Crichton. For the most part, over the decades, their portraits coalesce in European accounts so that all Sherpa characters appear as cheerful, tough, loyal, and brave – and always mountaineers. Every expedition book had to have one; very few authors moved past those famous smiles to the minds behind them.

In 1926, Rinchen Lhamo, a Tibetan woman who married a colonial official and settled in Britain, published *We Tibetans*, a response to Western versions of her homeland. 'Why should people write falsehoods about us, why should they write at all of things they do not know?' Rinchen Lhamo asked her readers. 'It is so much easier to say what is expected rather than what is true, but contrary to established views.' She wrote in the aftermath of John Noel's *The Epic of Everest*, and Noel's decision to hire Tibetan monks to appear on stage in an effort to boost ticket sales. Scenes of ordinary Tibetans picking fleas from each other's hair caused outrage among Tibetan aristocrats. What became known as the 'Affair of the Dancing Lamas' offered the authorities, Tibetan or British or both, a pretext to suspend climbing on Everest for a few years.

The Himalaya wasn't colonised in the way India was. But the steady drip of adventure stories, the accretion of fables passed on from one generation to the next, fixed in our minds a place that made no allowance for the turmoil of political and cultural change sweeping through the valleys at the height of their exploration. It was a sort of mythological acquisition. Foreign climbers photographed ancient faces, spoke of ancient cultures, even as their social fabric burst into flames. We wrote about the eternal snows, even as the glaciers began to disappear.

The few written accounts from early Sherpa climbers – only Tenzing Norgay and Ang Tharkay, the most successful *sirdars* – are mediated through Western co-authors and to some extent pander to this construct of a mythical race, even if, through the cracks, you can see a boiling frustration at how the Sherpas are sometimes treated, and an understandable desire to improve their working conditions. 'I do feel that in his story of our final climb he is not quite fair to me;' Tenzing Norgay explained through his ghost, 'that all the way through he indicates that when things went well it was his doing and when things went badly it was mine.'

Such historical baggage can be annoying for modern Sherpas who want to be accountants or dentists and who think climbing dangerous and unnecessary. Tashi Sherpa put it nimbly. 'I've relied on my sense of the absurd to find humour when non-Sherpas doubt that someone like me could manage a global business without the mentorship or patronage of some 'Western guru' to nurture my growth. Can we only be imagined as the uncomplaining second man with a pack on his back and crampons under his feet?' The Twitter feed of the protest blog Reclaiming Sherpa was more direct: 'Westerners do not have the right to box us into certain stereotypes, impose their meaning on us, trivialise the word that represents us, and then profit off of it … Dear cultural appropriators, you are our baggage. #Sherpafordummies.'

On the other hand, that baggage still incubates sympathy. The outpouring of concern for the bereaved families following the 2014 avalanche resulted in large donations to relief funds – hundreds of thousands of dollars. As the blogger Jemima Diki Sherpa wrote in the accident's aftermath: 'It is something to behold, the open-hearted enthusiasm that the Sherpa name elicits in the western mind.' No other ethnic group in Nepal – Gurkhas comprise several groups – has remotely the public profile Sherpas have in the West, even if that image is borrowed and warped.

Half an hour down the trail to base camp, a small group of non-Sherpa porters passed me, mostly young, one holding a smartphone to his ear, listening to music. They carried with them the tang of wood-smoke and kerosene and sweat, a scent that's ubiquitous in much of upland Nepal, but is fading from this part of Khumbu. Behind them was an old man, knees bowed, dressed in rags and carrying a basket – a *doko*. He straightened as he saw me and raised his right hand in greeting. I noticed the tip of his middle finger was missing, and then, when I looked harder, I saw that while the flesh had gone, the bone of his fingertip remained.

'What happened?' I asked waggling my own middle finger.

'Dhaulagiri,' he said, waggling his head. 'Frostbite.' I reached for my wallet, but he held up his hand again. 'No money. Just hello.' And then he smiled and walked on.

How many stories like this had I heard over the years, tales of loss and suffering and so often in the aftermath nothing – inadequate compensation, little compassion and no resolution. It was why I was in Nepal now: I'd been sent an email by a trekker who had spent a lot of time in the country. She had passed the bodies of two porters on her way to Mera Peak, not far from Everest, abandoned like garbage by their Nepali employer when they collapsed in the snow from altitude sickness. The region around Mera Peak's base camp is a notorious altitude trap; porters with altitude sickness are regularly sent back to the Hinku valley over the Mera La (5,410 metres), compounding their problems. Unlike Sherpas, other ethnic groups at work in the high Himalaya – Tamangs, Rais and Chhetris – have no genetic advantage to protect them. How, she wondered, could deaths like these still be occurring?

'They were probably Rai,' a friend in Kathmandu told me. 'The Sherpas say they're more prone to altitude sickness. Rais migrated from Burma so it's possible they're more susceptible.'

Rai settlements, such as Bung and Chheskam south of Mera Peak, provide a lot of the porters who still keep the trekking and climbing industry in Khumbu supplied and moving. That's work almost no Sherpas in Khumbu do any more. If they are still carrying loads, it's only on commercial climbing expeditions. Rais are also the farmhands working in the fields, the cooks in the kitchen and the stonemasons chipping blocks for construction. Their villages, without the infrastructure and comforts tourists demand, are very different places to Namche. If you're looking for invisible men and women, here they are. No one sends a film crew when porters from Chheskam don't come home from work.

I didn't know the names of the porters on Mera Peak, and I still don't; the deaths of the Sherpas and other high-altitude workers on Everest deflected me from my path. But even before the avalanche that April, I wondered how it could be that some deaths in Nepal's mountains resonate, prompting calls for change and promises of help, while others are met with a shrug or worse. I thought of a porter dying alone, his body only half-buried under wind-blown snow, abandoned so that someone's holiday wouldn't be delayed.

Who, I wondered, would educate his kids?

More than four decades ago, Peter Matthiessen arrived in Nepal with the zoologist George Schaller, half-broken with grief following the death of his young wife from brain cancer and clinging desperately to his new fascination with Buddhism, born, he said, from his experiments with acid. That year, 1973, Bill Tilman was sailing to Greenland, still puffing on his pipe and living on hardtack. By then, he'd devoted twenty years to the sea, after deciding the Himalaya had become too crowded. Eric Shipton was on his last significant expedition: the first ascent of Mount Burney in Patagonia. Like the pioneers, Matthiessen looked into the faces of his porters, and he thought he saw reflected back the very things he'd come looking for: mysticism, redemption, and more lasting and essential truths than those he'd discovered in America.

Few Himalayan travel books capture such dreams of transformation better than *The Snow Leopard*. When Matthiessen died, a few days before the avalanche on Everest, it was this book that obituary writers mentioned first, an inner journey every bit as dramatic as the landscapes he crossed with Schaller, a beguiling if selective tour of the 'secrets' of Buddhism. And yet, when it came to the people who lived in those landscapes, Matthiessen strayed into the kind of projections the Palestinian intellectual Edward Said warned against in *Orientalism*: 'The Orient is the stage on which the whole East is confined. On this stage will appear the figures whose role it is to represent the larger whole from which they emanate.'

This process is most obvious in Matthiessen's descriptions of the porter Tukten, an ex-Gurkha and veteran of expeditions that featured Chris Bonington, including the first ascent of the south face of Annapurna in 1970. Matthiessen depicts him as 'a wiry small man with Mongol eyes and outsized ears'. He admires Tukten's calm demeanour while at the same time wondering whether this 'red-faced devil' isn't out to destroy him. 'Whatever this man is – wanderer or evil monk, or saint or sorcerer – he seems touched by what Tibetans call the "crazy wisdom": he is free.'

Matthiessen noted that the younger Sherpas kept their distance from Tukten, while at the same being mesmerised by the older man's hypnotic storytelling. In one dramatic episode, during a mail run to Jumla, Tukten fought with Gyaltsen, another of the porters, and threatened to abscond to India with the letters. When he gets back to camp, the mail intact, Tukten answers Matthiessen's enquiries with a shrug, and Matthiessen is happy to let it go.

Concealed rage is a characteristic of *The Snow Leopard*; Matthiessen entertains violent fantasies about pulling the pigtails of his porters and smashing them in the face. But he imagines himself inextricably connected to them. 'It is not so much that this man and I are friends,' he wrote of Tukten at the book's conclusion. 'Rather, there is a thread between us, like the black thread of a live nerve; there is something unfinished, and he knows it, too. Without ever attempting to speak about it, we perceive life in the same way, or rather, I perceive it in the way that Tukten lives it.'

This is the truth Matthiessen stumbles over but never quite acknowledges: in saying that he wishes he could live life as 'his' Sherpa does, he really means he wishes he could live life more fully as himself. He has little idea of how Tukten actually lives, for he has never made more than a half-hearted effort to tear himself away from his grief and self-absorption to understand more fully the dynamics of his little band of porters, who in his estimation were either 'childlike' or sorcerers – and never working men carrying the needs of their families on their backs.

Had Matthiessen enquired, it's possible he would have discovered Tukten was not a Sherpa at all, but a Tibetan who had crossed the border, as many have done over the centuries, to find a better way of life. This might explain why the Sherpas in Matthiessen's group kept their distance. Tukten's lone-wolf status, his equanimity of spirit, his psychological resilience was not sorcery – it was the hallmark of the outsider.

Also missing from *The Snow Leopard* is any sort of historical context. That lacuna is understandable. Matthiessen's journey is personal and psychological; he's not writing a travelogue or taking the political air. But his journey did occur at a particular time, when Richard Nixon's rapprochement with China had abruptly curtailed American support for the Tibetan cause. A year after Matthiessen left Dolpo, some Tibetan freedom fighters committed suicide in neighbouring Mustang rather than surrender to the encircling Nepali army.

In the early 1950s, Indian independence and Nehru's defenestration of Nepal's corrupt Rana dynasty had lifted the dreams of Nepali democrats. By the early 1970s those dreams had congealed into disappointment. The monarchy had reasserted itself and Nepal's progress slowed in the sticky quagmire of the *panchayat* system of royal appointees. Not for nothing did Dervla Murphy call her book on Nepal *The Waiting Land*. Mountaineers photographed elongated lines of porters in bare feet or gym shoes snaking their way to base camps, gasping under the weight of their loads. They seemed resolute, steadfast; the reality was deference and fatalism in the face of centuries of oppression.

Matthiessen wasn't the last to fall into the trap of seeing only those things in the Himalaya he came to find. Most visitors do it. We read the famous stories; we look at images of spinning prayer wheels and robed monks and imagine an apparently timeless world where we can reconfigure ourselves. Like me, Ben Ayers read *The Snow Leopard* before he came to Nepal for the first time: 'I ended up going to Dolpo and tracing some of [Matthiessen's] steps. I liked the book and was influenced by this dharma-travel sort of idea. The notion that by experiencing other wild cultures, that wildness or enlightenment rubs off on you.'

I talked with Ben in the garden of his home on the outskirts of Kathmandu where he lived for several years, not far from the zoo. (The house was destroyed in the earthquake of 2015.) It's not uncommon, especially at night, to hear the tigers growling; visit during the weekend and for a few dollars you can feed them. When I first met Ben, in the mid 2000s at the Royal Geographical Society in London, he seemed impossibly young to be campaigning to improve the rights of porters in Nepal. He filled the lecture hall with zealous intensity, spoke Nepali fluently, and provoked in me a disagreeable emotion that I later identified as envy.

His hair is thinner now, his expression a little rueful at the memory of that night. He travelled to Nepal as a student because he was interested in mountaineering. 'I wasn't a terribly gifted climber but it was part of my identity and mountains were part of my growing up. Nepal occupied a place in my imagination, as it does for all of us. Then I came out here and it blew my mind.' Coming from a comparatively wealthy middle-class background in America, his instinct was to get involved. As a climber, he had grown up looking at photographs of smiling porters on their way to the mountains; they seemed the obvious place to start.

'When I saw someone carrying a load with a *namlo* – a tumpline across the forehead – it was so foreign to me yet so simple. It was such a basic form of labour, without any mechanical advantage, not even straps on a backpack. That seemed to me representative of Nepal, both its strength and its poverty.' Just before flying to Nepal, Ben had been studying the work of ethnologist and photographer Edward Sheriff Curtis, and had come across an image showing Native Americans carrying baskets with tumplines. (Matthiessen makes similar comparisons in *The Snow Leopard*.) 'So coming to Nepal was like stepping into a history book. It still is in some ways. Things happen here in ways that happened in Europe hundreds of years ago. Understanding *namlos* and portering became important to me.'

For many Americans and Europeans who explore the Himalaya, a sense of reconnection to our own history appears as a revelatory experience. We immerse ourselves in cultural nostalgia. The struggle towards modernity – along with its by-products of pollution and consumerism – seems less welcome. What we forget is the social progress, the votes won and the justice earned.

For Ben, it wasn't enough to observe. He had to participate. Having been turned down as a porter by every trekking agency in Thamel, he bluffed his way into the company of a small group of locals carrying rice for two and a half days to the village of Chainpur in eastern Nepal. These were supply porters, working for shopkeepers beyond the road-head and making a fraction of the pay a tourist porter earns. Ben has a strong frame, but he could barely manage forty kilos; the locals – honed from twice-daily meals of rice and dahl – carried 110, almost three times as much. 'It was fascinating and hard. It challenged me in so many different ways. These porters I was walking with were incredibly kind, incredibly funny and also incredibly intelligent. They were writing poems and singing songs.'

Ben laughed. 'I don't know where it came from,' he told me about his first years in Nepal, 'but I had picked up a terrible case of self-righteousness. Maybe it was being twenty.' He lived in Bhaktapur, the medieval town east of Kathmandu, on $75 a month, meeting with trades unions and talking to porters, trying to find out what they lacked. On the one hand they seemed incredibly tough, on the other horribly vulnerable. They lacked clothes for high altitude and shivered in caves or rough shelters at night. Without any adaptation to altitude they suffered illness at the same rates as tourists – more so, given the correlation between exertion and altitude problems. When they got sick they were dismissed, often without pay, so it was in their interest to hide altitude sickness, sometimes with fatal consequences. Education programs were cutting sickness rates among tourists – why not porters?

Ben crossed paths with the few others campaigning for better working conditions, such as the International Porters Protection Group, founded by Jim Duff who had been the doctor on Chris Bonington's 1975 Everest expedition. He then got a job at the Kathmandu Environmental Education Project, established in 1992 in memory of Tracey Taylor Young, a British climber who had died on her way down from Island Peak. She'd been in Khumbu to raise awareness about the damage being done by tourism.

Twenty years ago, when I first looked round KEEP's drop-in centre in Thamel, I had found their folksy message warmly inspiring; tourists were encouraged to eat *dal bhat* and not to take showers in water heated on a wood fire to stop deforestation – and to take care of porters. Now the good intentions seemed dusty and unheard, the old messages competing with the white noise of consumerism, good news from a lost world. A block down, one of my favourite cafes was full of fresh young tourist faces bent over smartphones looking for the best deals and posting selfies.

The visitor centre wasn't exactly buzzing in the late 1990s when Ben worked there. He filled his time pushing his agenda on porters' rights. Using his own money, he set up a small clothing bank. Then a BBC documentary-maker called Sangita Manandhar got in touch, wanting to cover the issue of porter deaths in the trekking industry. The film she made, *Carrying the Burden*, was a runner-up at Banff's film festival and toured North America, driving the issue into the open. Afterward, there were legal disputes over copyright, and in the kerfuffle, Ben left KEEP to set up his own non-profit called Porters' Progress. He moved to Lukla, gateway to Everest, and opened a new clothes bank. It was a shrewd location. The clothes would protect porters for the cold and high trek to Everest base camp and they more or less had to return to Lukla, making it easy to return what they borrowed.

Still in his early twenties, Ben found himself riding a dragon. His appearance in *Carrying the Burden* made him the point man for all the concern and indignation the film inspired. 'Malinda Chouinard [at Patagonia] called us up and said how can we help and we said, "Give us clothes." Suddenly we had all their seconds. We got stuff from North Face and Marmot. We had more gear than we knew how to handle. I wasn't a great fundraiser but I raised enough. Then we got a grant from the International Labour Organization to do child labour prevention. We started doing HIV classes and community development work in porter villages. We went from having four staff to twenty-four in less than a year. We became an NGO.'

Ben moved in with a Sherpa family in Chaurikharka, just down the hill from Lukla, where he began to confront the realities of modern Nepal. Porters' Progress was launched at the height of the civil war, and within a year Lukla became part of the front line. Maoist rebels attacked the airport. The king had declared a state of emergency in late 2001, and the authorities now established a garrison of soldiers and armed police to protect a valuable chunk of the tourist trade.

The gap between different ethnic groups and castes within Nepal widened during the civil war. In their struggle against the state and the Brahmins who ran it, the Maoists, whose own leadership was largely Brahmin, exploited existing ethnic tensions to garner allies. One of those fault lines occurs between Sherpas in Khumbu and communities to the south. True, Sherpas are on Everest through economic necessity, but most have left less lucrative forms of portering far behind. Some of those who own real estate on the Everest trail have become wealthy. The grand-kids and great-grandkids of the Sherpas who welcomed Charles Houston now run businesses in Kathmandu and Guangzhou. They drive cabs in Brooklyn and study in Europe. Shortly before he died, I had met John Hunt, leader of the 1953 Everest expedition, in a pub near his house in Oxfordshire. He was frail by then, and in elegiac mood. The subject got on to Edmund Hillary's Himalayan Trust. 'I warned Ed that singling out the Sherpas for special treatment would cause resentment.'

Born in Khumjung, Pema Sherpa now lives in Oregon, and after the Everest avalanche of 2014, she wrote a thoughtful column in a Kathmandu newspaper about what needed to change. There were familiar targets, principally the greedy and dysfunctional government, but she also raised the issue of how some wealthy Sherpas now profit from the risks under-taken by poorer Sherpas and by workers from other ethnic groups:

'If the same trekking owners who themselves were climbing Sherpas only decades ago are now willing to put other Sherpas into harm's way without adequate compensation and safety, then we as a society have the obligation to speak up. As Dr Martin Luther King Jr said: "History will have to record that the greatest tragedy of this period of social transition was not the strident clamour of the bad people, but the appalling silence of the good people." In the same way, if the majority of the Sherpas remain silent on this matter, they will be contributing to this abuse, and more deaths, and more tragedies.'

I wondered what reaction her article had prompted. 'What [feedback]

I did get reflected a tone of caution,' she told me. 'Any labour movement has risks, and speaking out can have consequences. This, combined with a Sherpa reticence to focus on difficulties and a Buddhist [and] cultural acceptance of what is, limited the flow.'

There's nothing exceptional in this reticence. How often do environmental or labour concerns get put to one side to protect business interests where you live? Pasang Yangjee Sherpa, an academic at Penn State University, told me: 'As a Sherpa woman and as an anthropologist, I see Sherpas as people with different socioeconomic backgrounds and different life experiences. Humans, regardless of which ethnic or racial group one belongs to, strive to make a better living for themselves and their families.' That's why we have society; it's why we allow governments to make decisions for the common good, so that family isn't all there is. Except that in Nepal, institutions, government and otherwise, are more often than not corrupt or incompetent.

In 2006 the Maoists moved into Lukla and demanded load restrictions and a minimum wage. They made Porters' Progress buy a set of scales to make sure the regulations were enforced. 'As much as the Maoists were problematic for me,' Ben said, 'they did in an afternoon what we couldn't do in seven years. It taught me about the importance and power of politics.' The Maoists knew precisely where the grievances lay that would garner them the most votes.

Such progress couldn't last. The war ended but was replaced with political stalemate. Some Maoists – *Maobadi* in Nepali – couldn't shake their old habits of extortion. Political and criminal classes bled into each other, creating what Nepalis wryly termed the *Khaobadi*, those who rob Nepal's beleaguered people to eat rather than fight for a new society. A drunk *goonda* from the Maoist youth wing got into a fight with a Lukla

Sherpa and came off badly. In retaliation, the Maoists called a porter strike and held a sit-in on the runway at Lukla airport. Any goodwill Porters' Progress had generated from five years of advocacy was dispersed in an instant. (The UK branch continues to raise money for projects but the organisation in Nepal is essentially moribund.)

No matter how it ended, Ben says it was worthwhile: 'I was involved in any number of cases of porters with frostbite, rescues, deaths, getting money for families – there was some good humanitarian advocacy. In the same way that people are now talking about the safety of Sherpas, we brought those questions up in people's minds about trekking. That was the best thing we did.'

He says his experiences during Nepal's civil war gave him the necessary insight for his next job, working for the dZi Foundation in the villages of porters he met in Lukla. 'The whole idea of letting communities drive projects came out of the conflict because we couldn't get to the villages to do it ourselves.' Although he is now out of porter advocacy, he still has optimism. 'If porters were paid decently, which wouldn't cost that much more, it could be a fantastic industry for Nepal. You ban the mules, or make them only for goods. And you treat porters as professionals. It's a job. We gave out books with a photo and their address and wrote down the trips they went on. It was good for selling their labour. The industry must become professionalised.'

Ten days after the young girl slipped a flower into my hand, I sat in the Namgyal Lodge in Machhermo, a *kharka*, or summer grazing place now studded with low buildings. Having crossed the Cho La alone that morning, I felt exhausted. I'd hired a porter in Lukla, apparently the only one left in the village. His name was Suman. Both his parents were dead and he lived with his uncle and aunt. Scrawny and young, he seemed ill equipped for any world, let alone the one he inhabited.

He dawdled on the first day, playing constantly with his phone. He told me he was sixteen, studying for his leaver's certificate at school and trying to make some extra cash for his fees. At least he was still in education. Outside Lukla, I'd watched nine-year-olds carry loads toward Namche; child labour is theoretically illegal in Nepal but plenty of children skip school to bring in extra income. On the third morning, after a cold night at Tengboche, Suman wondered whether I might like to carry more of my gear. His load dropped from around twelve kilos to eight; the legal limit for a trekking porter is thirty. Later that morning, as a large group of people crossed the Dudh Kosi, a small stone fell from the steep bank and struck Suman a glancing blow on the head.

He touched his scalp and looked at his hand. 'Blood!' His knees sagged a little, and I helped him up the far bank where I examined the wound. It needed stitches, so I cleaned him up as best I could, covered the ragged flesh in gauze and wrapped duct tape around his head. Then, putting his rucksack into mine, I took him to the Himalayan Rescue Association health post at Pheriche. Suman stood on the scales so Edith, a volunteer doctor from the Netherlands, could calculate how much local anaesthetic to give him. I discovered I weighed twice as much as him. He curled up on the treatment table and took out his phone to listen to Nepali pop songs while Edith gently closed his wound.

'Well done for bringing him in,' she said.

'What else would I do?' I felt bad enough hiring him in the first place.

'Often they just get sent down on their own.'

'By tourists?'

'Nepalis too.'

While Suman dozed, I sat in a nearby lodge and watched a small group of Rai porters walk past the window with black film-gear cases the size of boulders hanging off their *namlos*. They were bringing down the gear for the NBC film crew who had been at Everest to record the exploits of wingsuit flier Joby Ogwyn. The porters were carrying triple loads totalling at least ninety kilos to make extra cash while the going was good. More porters were carrying similar loads for film crew arriving to film the grieving families of dead Sherpas. In all the heated debate about the morality of what happened on Everest, almost nobody had mentioned the welfare of men like these.

I thought of the cold at base camp, considered Suman's wafer-thin jacket, compared him to the tough-looking lads I'd just seen and walked to the health post to pay him off for the full twelve days I'd promised him. His replacement was a barrel-chested Rai called Mohan who picked up my twelve-kilo bag in one hand, waggled his head happily and disappeared up the trail to Lobuche, a day's walk from base camp. We agreed to meet at 7 a.m. next morning but by 8 a.m. he hadn't appeared. Another porter at the ramshackle lodge they'd shared sipped his tea and then tilted his chin towards base camp. 'He's gone to Everest. Many loads.' Mohan had calculated that if he went early to base camp, where expeditions were starting to leave, he could get three times the pay I was offering. Giving up on the notion of hiring local labour, I picked up my rucksack and walked on.

All this I explained to the middle-aged man sitting across the table from me at the Namgyal Lodge. His name was Ratna Tamang and he was guiding two South African women. 'You see,' Ratna said, 'now many people are going abroad to work. Migrant workers. It is not so easy to find porters now.'

No one knows for certain how many Nepalis are living and working in foreign countries because there's an open border with India, but it must be at least a fifth of the population. Sixteen hundred Nepalis leave Kathmandu's airport every day in search of jobs abroad. Much of Nepali life now revolves around money wired home from family members. Often, these workers have sunk themselves in debt to loan sharks to meet the costs of the employment agencies which find them work, and often abuse them too. More than a third of the country's GDP is earned this way, and as the money sluices through the banks, the government takes its own cut. When the Nepali investigative journalist Deepak Adhikari looked at the issue, he called his piece 'Bigger cages, longer chains'.

The manpower shortage in the mountains has been plugged by bringing in gangs of porters from villages several districts away – a workforce that finds it difficult to leave, just as they do in the Gulf. A Nepali friend who runs treks told me he had the number of a porter 'broker' who offered workers at fixed prices, either 'wet' or 'dry' depending on whether or not they would be fed. He told me the price per man per day – around eight dollars. I winced. Even with this migrant labour, the increasing use of mules in Khumbu is a strong indication that the old patterns of portering are breaking down. The margins on treks are better if you take the human factor out of it. But jobs are disappearing.

Ratna appeared content to stay in Nepal to work as a trekking guide. He liked meeting people, he said, and his South African clients seemed just as delighted with him. Trekking was not what he wanted for his children though. 'I want them to have better English,' he said, 'then they can work as tour guides in Kathmandu. Much more money.'

Next to him on the carpeted bench was their porter, Birdhan Rai, who sat with his hands folded in his lap and a smile on his face. Without any English, he couldn't move up the next rung on the trekking ladder to become a porter-guide. I couldn't stop looking at him, a potentially awkward habit since we had no language in common. There's a phrase in Nepali, *Rai ko ris*, 'the anger of Rais', that catches the stereotype often associated with Rais as cheerful but with explosive tempers. Like all such epithets, it is sometimes derogatory, especially used by outsiders, but can be worn with pride; it was, for example, the name of a feisty anarcho-punk band led by Sareena Rai.

Portering is part of life across Nepal but is often considered a little shameful; it's what you do if you've got nothing else. In the nineteenth century, Tamang populations north of Kathmandu had no choice in labouring for the city's ruling families, including working as porters on historic trade routes into Tibet. When they'd met their obligations, they carried timber or potatoes to market towns like Trisuli Bazaar – but only if they needed the cash. Not needing to porter was a sign you were doing okay. When anthropologist Ben Campbell asked Tamangs in the 1990s how they were doing economically, he wrote how 'the replies were often given to me precisely in the idiom of whether they did, or did not, have to engage in paid portering … More fatalistically, I was told that "some people are born to happiness, others to carry loads".'

Portering is also deeply embedded in Rai culture – 'a matter of pride' one researcher told me, although as with Tamangs, it's the pride coal-miners take in their work, while hoping their kids do better. Rais are famous for the scale of their loads, and they are the only group to use a *tokma*, a shaped wooden stick to prop their baskets on. Long before the tourists came, Rais would trek from their villages down to Ghurmi to buy salt or fabric, trade that for oranges, take those to the market at Namche to swap for potatoes and return home.

I was newly fascinated by their religion. Traditionally, Rais are neither Hindus nor Buddhists, but Kirantis, although some have converted over the years. Their rituals are focused on sacred landscapes, which tie them to earlier generations and are conducted through shamans. Rais take actual physical journeys around the power places of these landscapes, but they can also be conducted through them figuratively, reconnecting to their origins in time and space through the imagination.

Unable to say a word to Birdhan, however, I was reduced, like most travellers here, to speculation about this man's inner life. As tourists, we take fragments, chance encounters, misheard information, and con-fabulate, at times whipping up a palatable version of the world from the strangest ingredients. There is so much we don't see. How *sirdars*, who organise porters, pocket a percentage of their wages. How sick porters get sent down alone, or aren't paid. When I asked Ben Ayers if trekkers should be better educated, he shook his head. 'Tourists are ignorant catalysts. It's not feasible to educate them enough to make judgements. They're not in a position to demand anything. When you stay in a hotel, can you look into the lives of the people laundering the towels?'

Where tourists can make an impact is in demanding ethical practices from businesses they hire. Several Western trekking companies I spoke to already have porter welfare sewn into their business model, while acknowledging that making it stick is difficult when so many sharp practices are hard to spot. The International Porter Protection Group, widely regarded as a positive force for change, has five guidelines for porter welfare. Dr Nick Mason from IPPG told me: 'Anybody using a commercial company to trek or climb in Nepal should ask whether these guidelines are followed and if they are not explain to the company why they are going elsewhere.' Whether young tourists on a budget, embarking on what may prove to be the only trek of their lives, feel able to turn down a cheap deal is another matter.

Next morning, I visited the IPPG health post and porters' shelter on the edge of Machhermo. After years of dispensing healthcare from lodges, this purpose-built facility opened in 2006, built and run by the IPPG and staffed with volunteer doctors in the spring and autumn seasons. This year's volunteers were helping oversee a new post under construction in Gokyo, a day's walk up the trail. They were in the garden sunbathing when I arrived, and though warmly welcoming, I felt I was interrupting a ship's crew who had been at sea for months. They were all sharply intelligent, picking apart the flaws and abuses in the trekking industry, the wobbly scaffolding that propped it up, which tourists rarely glimpsed. Emily was the youngest, a medical student in her early twenties with a sardonic sense of humour. 'It *might* help,' she said, as she described the chronic overloading of porters, 'if they had some scales at Lukla.' I wondered what had happened to the set Porters' Progress had bought.

The health post kept records of the porters they treated, semi-formal interviews that accreted into a dataset of hard labour and modest dreams. Each entry was a small biography, of farms too small to yield enough of a living, of the bitter cold at high altitude and of hopes for their kids. There were teenage boys and old men, one or two on their first job, most of them veterans. Some had worked in Malaysia or the Gulf and some of them were hoping to get back there for the higher wages. One porter spent the rest of the year as a stonemason. He'd said: 'Portering is easier than breaking rocks.'

Most spoke of the soaring cost of food in Khumbu, where increasing transportation costs compound normal inflation. Campaigners had told me, and the doctors confirmed, that some porters couldn't afford two meals a day in the upper reaches of popular trekking areas. I tried to imagine what it would be like to carry thirty kilos at 4,500 metres on one bowl of rice and lentils – and what might happen if the weather turned bad to someone who wasn't eating properly. The cost of living was so high that many relied on tips from tourists to make up their wages, an option only open to those with direct access to foreigners. Supply porters, those carrying bottles of beer and packets of noodles for trekkers to consume, are allowed to carry more weight, the only way they can make something approaching a living wage. I came across only one porter – a younger man – who preferred this work for that reason.

Returning to the Namgyal, I stepped over the team of workers tapping away at rocks for the walls of a new bathroom. Like the kitchen workers, none of them were Sherpas. The boy behind the desk was a Tibetan exile who told me about his mother and how he feared he'd never see her again. That evening in the Namgyal, I watched the owner welcome a group of German trekkers to his lodge. Their outfitting company, judging by the number of its stickers left around the walls, was a regular client. Each trekker was given a hot towel. We looked on enviously as they rubbed their faces. Then I noticed their porters creeping into the dining room. The owner herded the porters to a table away from the rest of us, where they sat crammed together, mostly staring at the table, sometimes whispering to each other. Once they had wolfed down their food, they stood up and meekly filed out.

Back in England, a few minutes' drive from my house in Sheffield, I met Padam Simkhada. Padam was born in Dhading in Nepal, not far from Pokhara below the Annapurna region. He was, when I met him, a senior lecturer in public health at Sheffield Hallam University with an academic interest in the health of porters and guides. In 2010 he'd co-authored an eye-opening report on sexual behaviour among trekking guides, revealing an otherwise hidden world of lodges providing sex workers for male tourists and trekking guides and sexual relations between trekking guides and female clients. ('If they are beautiful then we want to have sex with them,' one guide had told him. 'Otherwise we do it for money.') All twenty-one guides interviewed knew where there were sex workers on the trails they walked.

Padam seemed almost bewildered by the pace of change in Nepal. 'Every time I go back there are things I don't recognise.' Poverty, that weighty, galvanising terror, drives everything. Construction is booming, fuelled by a rising population on the move, sending money home from abroad. Villages are emptying as men and women from all corners of society migrate for work. 'The elite head for Europe, North America and Japan,' Padam said, and he smiled at the irony of his own position. 'The next group down heads to Malaysia and Korea then the Gulf. Workers need to borrow £800 or £900 to get there. After six years they've barely paid back the moneylenders. And when they go, the families find it easier to get more loans, putting families in more debt. There's no advice on how to manage remittances for those left behind.'

This vast social upheaval is changing the porter industry just as it is every other aspect of Nepali society. Construction of dirt roads brings buses and trucks to villages that were once supplied by porters, removing their chance for a wage and driving them to seek work elsewhere. 'Shop-keepers aren't bothered,' Padam said. 'Their goods become cheaper.' Padam could remember as a child on his way to school being carried across a river by a local Magar man his parents knew – a local man performing an essential service for his community. That aspect of Nepali life is fading now. Farming children used to have a small basket and a short *namlo* and carry little loads, young apprentices to a life of toil. Today's kids with their mobile phones and city dreams won't tolerate such narrow horizons any more.

'Tourism may preserve portering,' Padam told me, 'because of the higher wages. It's still a profitable business. Undergraduates work as porters with hopes of becoming a guide. It offers a career ladder.' Climbing that ladder is still a perilous journey. Padam ticked off the threats posed in an industry that has chronically failed to regulate itself properly: inadequate clothing, inadequate food, the lack of training, isolation from families, drug and alcohol abuse in a country where deaths from contaminated home brew are routine. No one knows exactly how many Nepalis die in the trekking and climbing industry each year; no one in government is counting and deaths often go unrecorded.

As I wrote this, the tail end of Cyclone Hudhud dumped feet of snow on the Annapurna region. The storm was forecast but in the rush to make money not enough people in the trekking business paid sufficient atten-tion. The Thorung La, a familiar sell to Thamel backpackers looking for a cheap trek, became a death zone. Of the official death toll of forty-three, likely to be higher, twenty-two were local guides and porters. As so often happens, it was some of the poorest in Nepal who paid the ultimate price, not those profiting from their labour. Ben Campbell, writing in the 1990s about one ethnic group, the Tamangs, explained how the division of labour in Nepal had shifted a little with the advent of trekking, how some Sherpas had profited from the sudden popularity of their homeland. 'But the overall structure is one that only has a role for Tamangs as human beasts of burden. The details may have changed, but the Tamangs are still carrying loads to make profits for the Kathmandu elite.'

Campbell could have been writing about any of the dispossessed and powerless struggling to make a living in the Himalaya. Nepal's long climb from impoverished servitude to mutual respect and social justice has only just begun. Trekking and mountaineering bring millions of revenue to the Himalaya. Too often, organisations charged with using that money for the benefit of workers don't do their job properly. Too often, porter trades unions ignore the injustices their members endure. What should we do about it? As mountain lovers, climbers or trekkers, we have a responsibility to those we employ, directly or indirectly. We should open our eyes to the poor regulation and open corruption that plagues this industry, and not just write a cheque to charity and continue in our own myths.

At the time of writing, there has been no enquiry into what happened on Annapurna, or any appeal for the families of the trekking guides and porters who died in October 2014. Like the two dead men I'd been told about on Mera, I couldn't even find a list of their names.

Wanderers, saints and sorcerers – working men, sons and fathers – they had simply vanished.

What's Eating
Ueli Steck?

2014

As convention centres go, Chamonix's Le Majestic is right up there. Located in a former belle époque hotel opened in 1913, rooms that once thronged with Europe's ritziest socialites have been sumptuously restored. Outside, the last light of a beautiful day glows pink on the summit of Mont Blanc. Inside, a ruck of journalists, publicists, photographers and local bigwigs are loading up at the buffet and chatting in small groups.

Mixed into this low-rent crowd, like unicorns stumbling through a herd of goats, are several of the world's greatest mountaineers, gathered for alpinism's annual awards ceremony, the Piolets d'Or. Across the room I spot the unmistakable jawline – like a Habsburg prince – of Hansjörg Auer, one of Europe's newest stars whose glittering alpine résumé features hard new routes in Patagonia and the Karakoram as well as rock climbs up to 8b+ in the Dolomites.

Nearby are his brother Matthias – similarly chinned – and Simon Anthamatten, the other two members of last year's expedition to the south-west face of Kunyang Chhish East (7,400 metres); they are among the nominees for this year's prize. There's something pleasingly boyish about Anthamatten. Now thirty, he looks ten years younger despite being a veteran of several Himalayan expeditions. Maybe it's the tousled blond hair. I watch him try – and fail – to stifle a yawn.

Anthamatten won a Piolet d'Or in 2008 for the first ascent of the steep north face of Tengkangpoche that looms over Nepal's Khumbu valley. His partner on that occasion, Ueli Steck, is in the room too, surrounded by a knot of admirers, smiling, nodding, eyes shining, and absolutely not yawning. Steck seems to thrive on this contact with the public. You wouldn't guess he's in the middle of the worst crisis of his high-profile career. You can't tell that behind the smiles his greatest achievement – and one of the greatest in mountaineering's history – has been called into question.

In October 2013, Steck soloed a new line on the gigantic south face of Annapurna in just twenty-eight hours. Given the history of the face in general and that route in particular, the climb was big news, sealing his reputation as one of the greatest alpinists ever. Yet when they heard the full story, many of his peers began expressing doubts, Hansjörg Auer among them. Steck had no proof of his ascent, and his account to journalists contained errors of fact and inconsistencies. Sceptics pointed to the lack of documentary evidence, a regular feature of Steck's career despite his high-profile sponsors.

'There are also people who doubt the moon landings,' Steck told the Swiss news outlet *Berner Zeitung*, in an interview soon after the climb. 'I don't care; I did Annapurna for me, not for someone else.' Despite such protests, the Piolets d'Or clearly means something to Steck, if only to show he has no reason to hide.

What Steck means to the Piolets d'Or is another matter. Even at the best of times the Piolets d'Or are controversial. But they do, at least according to director Christian Trommsdorff, offer a chance for the media to talk about something other than Everest. 'We want something positive from the Piolets d'Or,' said Catherine Destivelle, one of the judges for 2014. So October's news from Annapurna seemed an ideal opportunity. It was the sort of climb that might appeal to the judging panel's president, George Lowe. Hold the criteria of the Piolets d'Or – style, commitment, creativity and respect – against Lowe's record in the 1970s, especially his famous attempt on Latok I's north ridge with Jim Donini, Jeff Lowe and Michael Kennedy, and you had the perfect match. Steck's climb was a similar landmark in the history of alpinism.

His nomination for a Piolet was inevitable, his chances of winning high. But his nomination had caused a thumping headache for the organisers and proved contentious with at least some of the jury. Because lying in the judges' inbox was a sheaf of emails from alpinists and journalists on both sides of the Atlantic questioning Steck's ascent. His claimed route on Annapurna was just the kind of achievement the Piolets was set up to honour. If Steck's a faker, then his nomination would be a blow to the award's reputation.

But it went far deeper than that. The Swiss climber isn't an outsider, or a peripheral figure; he's at the core of the sport's image around the world. This wasn't just an attack on one of modern climbing's brightest stars; it called into question the whole status of high-grade mountaineering as it is practised now, and the role of the circus that follows it – the sponsors, journalists and film-makers.

Simply put, if Ueli Steck is rotten, what does that say about alpinism?

If you were drawing up a list of sublime mountaineering challenges, then the south face of Annapurna would be near the top. Three miles wide and a mile and a half high, it's a wall of white and gold that starts steep and gets steeper at a near-vertical rock band at 7,000 metres. The face is divided into three equidistant buttresses, each of them climbed in a ten-year period that began in 1970 when a British team – led by Chris Bonington – put Don Whillans and Dougal Haston on the summit via the left-hand pillar. Like the British, the Japanese and Polish expeditions that climbed the central and right-hand buttresses used siege-style tactics – big teams hauling loads up fixed ropes to camps – to overcome their objectives. Then, in the early 1980s, the alpine-style revolution got underway.

In 1982, Alex MacIntyre and the Franco-Italian René Ghilini set out to climb a ramp trending up and left from the right side of the right-hand pillar.

They took just three pitons and an ice screw, and while retreating from unexpectedly blank rock at over 7,000 metres, MacIntyre was struck on the head by a single stone falling from high on the face. He died instantly.

Two years later, in 1984, the Catalans Enric Lucas and Nil Bohigas, barely known outside their native country, completed the line. They took a bigger rack than MacIntyre and Ghilini and found they needed it. Starting at night to reduce the risk of loose stones on the lower face, they spent a whole day in the rock band covering just fifty metres in two pitches. Overall they graded the route at V+ and A2 with eighty-degree ice. It took five bivouacs to reach Annapurna's central summit. Then, using their eighty-metre, seven-millimetre ropes, they abseiled the Polish route in just eighteen hours.

It was a dazzling achievement, full of the elan and commitment that is the hallmark of alpine style. Thirty years on, the Catalan route is still held up as a gold standard in mountaineering. Their ascent also riveted the attention of other climbers to the centre of Annapurna's south wall. Could something also be done in alpine style up there?

France's leading alpinist Pierre Béghin thought so, and in 1992 attempted a new line, the eventual route, more or less, of Steck's ascent in 2013, between the British and Japanese pillars. Climbing with Jean-Christophe Lafaille, on his first Himalayan expedition, they had almost overcome the rock band – and with it the most difficult climbing – when they were hit by a storm. Abseiling back through the band, Béghin settled his weight on to a badly placed cam; the gear ripped and he disappeared into space. Lafaille was left to down-climb on his own. During his epic descent, stonefall broke his arm.

Completing the Béghin-Lafaille route has been an obvious challenge for the world's elite. Christian Trommsdorff, for example, took a look in 2000 with Yannick Graziani and Patrick Wagnon. (A well-known team who often climbed together, their initials – TGW – make a pun on

France's high-speed trains, the TGV.) Graziani went with Stéphane Benoist for another look in 2010; these two would be back on the peak in the autumn of 2013.

Ueli Steck himself had two goes, the first – in 2007 – by himself. Soloing up at 5,800 metres, he was struck on the helmet by a rock and knocked out, falling 300 metres. Coming to, he wandered around the glacier, discombobulated with concussion, until a team member found him. Steck went back again in 2008 with Simon Anthamatten, his partner from Tengkangpoche, but the pair abandoned their climb to help Spanish climber Iñaki Ochoa, marooned high on the east ridge having suffered a stroke.

This rescue attempt, which involved several others including Don Bowie and Denis Urubko, proved dangerous, protracted and harrowing for Steck. He behaved, by anyone's measure, with courage and ingenuity. It culminated with Steck on his knees in a small tent at 7,400 metres, driving a syringe of dexamethasone into Ochoa's thigh, having climbed up alone in a pair of borrowed high-altitude boots. In some places the snow had been chest deep.

Ochoa, who had been tent-bound for days and was probably suffering from pulmonary oedema, was too weakened for Steck's intervention to work. Despite a second injection the following day, he died at noon. Steck stayed with him until the end and helped Ochoa's Romanian partner put the body in a nearby crevasse. Then, in poor visibility, he led the way down in poor weather using the GPS he'd been loaned for the ascent. Anthamatten had needed to explain to Steck, who had never used a GPS, how it worked.

Afterwards, Ochoa's brother Pablo expressed his gratitude for the efforts of all those involved in the rescue attempt: 'They are great examples to the rest of us.'

The bare bones of Ueli Steck's successful Annapurna climb, from his own account, are this: On 8 October 2013, with his partner Don Bowie, Steck set out for their Camp 1 on the south face, at 6,100 metres. At the bergschrund, Bowie, who had already expressed misgivings about this particular route, told Steck he would not be going on. After thinking it through, Steck decided to continue.

His reasoning was this: he had already been to 6,800 metres while acclimatising, and didn't want to return to base camp without achieving something, even if that meant more acclimatisation. He knew that the weather would soon shut down. He also knew that the two French climbers, Benoist and Graziani, would soon be back from their acclimatisation peak and that he had the option of joining them. He would go and take a look and see what happened. Bowie and the photographer Dan Patitucci, who had also walked up, retreated to a safe distance and waited to offer Steck moral support until he reached Camp 1. After they saw Steck arrive there, they descended to advance base camp.

Steck says he reached Camp 1 at around 9 a.m. and stopped for a short time while he repacked his rucksack. He was impressed by conditions. At the bergschrund, previously a six-metre rock step, he discovered avalanches had filled the gap, and he front-pointed straight up. The snow, as he describes it, was squeaky névé.

Looking up he could see it was windy. On Annapurna's south face that means spindrift avalanches. He knew he wouldn't be going on to the rock band in those conditions and was in no immediate hurry. He packed his rucksack with his tent, a stove, a little food, a sixty-metre, six-millimetre rope, some pitons – he says five – and a couple of ice screws. Then he continued to the headwall, reaching around 7,000 metres in the middle of the afternoon. With the wind still strong, he decided to put up his tent and wait until dusk, knowing that the wind would most likely moderate when the sun left the face. He spotted a likely looking spot, protected by rock above, but when he got there he discovered blue ice under the snow and there was no chance of digging a platform.

Although thwarted from pitching the tent, his position did give him an excellent view of the rock band and his route up it. He decided to take a photo: 'When I stopped to take the picture I realised how white the headwall was,' he told me. 'I was a little bit at the side and I could see the structure. It's not a vertical face. There seemed to be a line linking together, up snow and ice runnels.'

Soon after, before he could put his camera away, he claims a spindrift avalanche struck him, tearing away one of his mittens – and his camera. There would be no pictures. 'I almost got swept off the face,' he said. 'But [the incident] changed my mind. Before I was being quite casual, thinking I'll go have a look.' This near miss, he says, left him determined to try the headwall.

Knowing he would have to wait until sunset, he climbed down for a hundred metres before discovering a crevasse he could shelter in. Don Bowie said he watched Steck disappearing into this crevasse before cloud and mist obscured the view. Around dusk, some time between 5 p.m. and 6 p.m. in the early evening, the wind dropped as predicted and Steck started climbing again. (He has been somewhat inconsistent about exactly when this happened. Sunset on 8 October was at 5.42 p.m.) The exceptional snow conditions Steck says he found meant he was able to make rapid progress through the technically demanding rock band. When Graziani and Benoist later came the same way on 21 October they reported thin ice on vertical ground, with pitches up to ninety degrees. But by then, warm temperatures had stripped the thick white ice and névé that had allowed Steck to move so quickly.

Steck says he was at the summit at around 1 a.m., spent a few minutes there, then began his descent. 'Before the expedition I trained a lot for down-climbing [including a solo down-climb of the *1938 Route* on the Eiger], because of the whole story of Béghin and Lafaille. In my head, if Lafaille hadn't been able to down-climb he'd be dead.' Reversing the headwall, Steck used Abalakovs or V-threads to make a number of rappels on his six-millimetre rope, feeding the cord directly through – leaving no webbing behind.

Don Bowie woke 'just after first light' on 9 October, hearing movement and Dan Patitucci talking with Steck's friend and base camp manager Tenji Sherpa outside the tents. (Dawn on 9 October was at 6 a.m.) 'I heard them say they could see him down climbing so I immediately got dressed,' Bowie said. Steck was roughly at the point where they had seen him the previous night. According to Patitucci's blog Tenji said to him: 'My dream was that Ueli stood on the summit last night.' Patitucci suggested he might be able to see footprints on the summit, through the 500mm lens – plus doubler – on his camera.

In his account, Patitucci was unclear on whether he looked for Steck during the night or how often. On his Facebook page, he wrote: 'We couldn't sleep and so stayed up searching the wall, hoping to see something.' Yet his blog about that night contradicts this version in the first line. 'Ueli … my first thought upon waking.' (Perhaps surprisingly for a professional photographer, Patitucci didn't set up a camera to record the face while he slept. 'I never thought [of it]. It's not my thing. I have been asked repeatedly why I didn't do a time-lapse. I don't even know how to do one.')

Don Bowie said he got out of his tent 'a couple of times' in the night to look for Steck. On the first occasion, at around midnight, the face was shrouded by mist. Then, in the early hours and with the face now clear, he heard Tenji walking around outside. Tenji asked him if he could see a light. 'I told Tenji that you won't see a light from that distance. No way with a naked eye would you see a headlamp. With a 500mm lens with doubler he was just a dot. He was at least three kilometres distant, maybe three kilometres to four kilometres away and two kilometres to three kilometres higher.' When Bowie stuck his head out this time, he saw only the dark south face of Annapurna.

In the morning, according to Patitucci, Bowie said he'd received a text message from Steck in the night saying: 'I am back in Camp 2. Long night climbing. I am descending after some food.' Despite this, Bowie and Patitucci still had no idea of whether Steck had reached the summit. Once Steck had been located, Bowie suggested they hike up to meet him as he reached the glacier. Tenji packed some food and drink – bread, an apple and a Coke. When they found each other, Steck told Bowie that they could go home now. He'd reached the summit.

To Bowie, Steck's success was bittersweet. Like Steck, Bowie had rounded up sponsors and he felt an obligation to them. While the line Steck took up the face had been too difficult for him to climb mostly unroped, he had hoped that the two could do one of Annapurna's more modest lines and go home with something. Now, for him, the trip was a bust. 'I can say in a real honest reflection that part of me was relieved that I wouldn't have to get on the wall again,' Bowie said, 'part was upset that I wouldn't get to get on the face, and part of me was so proud of his accomplishment, and knew that we had just witnessed something extraordinary.'

If you take Ueli Steck's account of his climb at face value, then it certainly is one of the most extraordinary ascents ever made. Steck himself has downplayed the technical difficulty as 'not such a big deal'. The Catalans thirty years ago, he says, faced similar ground. But the mental control and fitness required to solo a vast wall like that and at such speed is still astonishing.

Yet by the time Steck was back in Switzerland, the gasp of collective amazement at his feat had given way to scepticism among some of his peers. When climbers and journalists began to pick over the details, there didn't seem to be a shred of evidence to support the claim. In fact, to some of them Steck's feat seemed, quite literally, incredible. Rumours circulated that the violence on Everest earlier in the year, when Sherpas had threatened Steck at Camp 2, had prompted some kind of breakdown, that he needed success on Annapurna to find closure – or placate his sponsors.

Was it really possible that Steck had climbed to the summit at 8,091 metres from 6,900 metres, up such technical ground, in the dark, and then reversed all that ground and more in just twelve hours? And only seventeen days after arriving at base camp? Graziani and Benoist, who repeated the route two weeks later, spent ten days on the face. Two were lost to bad weather, but two days were needed to get through the rock band and the Frenchmen reported vertical ground on both rock and ice. Conditions were undoubtedly different, but could they be *that* different?

Like mushrooms on rotten wood, doubts and inconsistencies began sprouting all over Steck's account. Why, as Patitucci reported, did he send a text to Don Bowie via satellite phone in which he said he'd been climbing all night but made no mention of the summit? And what about the GPS tracker on his wrist? This was a feature of his watch given to him by his sponsor Suunto, something he's effectively paid to wear, a device he had praised in a video made for Suunto. Steck didn't bother to switch it on, even briefly at the summit. Why not? Critics pointed to Steck's previous form for not documenting his climbs, notably a lightning-fast ascent of Shishapangma in 2011, when he climbed the 2,000-metre south-west face in just ten and a half hours. On that occasion, Steck said, his camera battery died.

Besides this lack of proof, there were inconsistencies in his account of Annapurna, particularly the different number of rappels he needed to descend the rock band. Was it a few? Or five? Or eight? Steck offered all three at different times to different people. Most damning was the interview he gave to the Swiss newspaper *Berner Zeitung*: 'There were four people at [advance] base camp who followed my every move with telescopes. Next day you could see my tracks in the snow.' But Steck's team hadn't been following his 'every move' and when Bowie and Patitucci had checked in the night they could find no trace of him.

Patitucci had noticed what looked like a track in the snow up high. He said: 'We only saw it when we first woke; it traversed the upper summit slope. We didn't remember seeing it the previous days, but the morning of Ueli's summit night, there it was, as the first sun hit the mountain. It was a part of the story as we all wondered what it was. But we assumed it had to be a crown; we couldn't imagine seeing Ueli's track from that distance, but we thought that maybe it was.'

Doubts expressed by some of the leading alpinists in the German-speaking world coalesced around the Vienna-based journalist Andreas Kubin, who eventually published his findings on the website *Bergsteigen*. (He says that two German magazines turned down the story for being too contentious.) At the bottom of the piece he thanked a number of prominent alpinists, including Hansjörg Auer and Stephan Siegrist. The inclusion of Siegrist's name on the list of doubters was a blow for Steck. The men had been friends and climbing partners.

Several names on the list preferred to stay off the record about their doubts when I contacted them. One told me: 'Public opinion would stone me as the old, jealous and crabby climber. That's why it cannot be an active climber but much more the media or an elder statesman who could make it public. In my opinion, it would be the obligation of responsible alpine journalism.'

Siegrist was more direct and open: 'I met Ueli on more than one occasion after his ascent of Annapurna. Ueli is a strong alpinist and as his friend, I believe him. However as an objective mountaineer I have my doubts. Like many other climbers, I have many questions about the ascent; the facts don't really add up. Ultimately the most important point is the outcome of the situation and the repercussions of Ueli's Annapurna ascent on the generations of alpinists to come. We need to establish parameters by which we can set reference points in alpinism. It's the only way to ensure new talent has a fair chance and isn't being pushed by levels of achievements we can't even prove actually exist. Without valid reference points the future of alpinism will become a mess.'

The scale of these doubts about Steck's Annapurna climb, so widespread and insistent, was a problem for Christian Trommsdorff and the Piolets d'Or jury. 'The questions are reasonable because Ueli Steck is a professional mountaineer and, even if there is no money involved in the Piolets d'Or, the win may lead to commercial benefits and media coverage,' Trommsdorff told the French newspaper *Le Monde*. When I caught up with him in Chamonix a few days before the award, he seemed exasperated by Steck's failure to record his climb: 'You're a pro in everything else, why not in measuring what you do? You cannot use the media only when you want to.'

Catherine Destivelle, one of the jury members, told me she was also unhappy with the lack of evidence for Steck's climb. 'I said to the jury that we have no real proof. But it's not in the charter of the Piolets d'Or, and the rest of the jury were surprised by my demand. They told me that they have no proof that he didn't do it. But we should have proof; this is the only sport where we don't need to show anything.'

Despite the intense speculation, Steck hadn't gone to ground. The day before the Piolets d'Or winners were announced, I met him at La Maison Carrier, a smart restaurant on the edge of town tastefully styled with timbers reclaimed from a simpler era.

Steck is physically neat, with a warm smile and clear blue eyes framed by long lashes. He is charming and often self-deprecating, qualities some of his peers regard with suspicion but endear him to audiences. Although I am one of many journalists he's due to meet before the ceremony, he is absolutely focused and unfailingly polite. For someone dubbed the 'Swiss Machine,' a nickname he is said to hate, he seems very human.

He immediately acknowledges the lack of evidence for his climb: 'I told [Andreas] Kubin from the start I don't have a summit picture. I've never tried to hide anything. I accept I have to be more careful in the future. I take that. But I can't change what happened in the past.'

I ask him if the media firestorm that erupted on Everest that spring had put him under pressure to do something positive. 'Leaving Everest in that way affected me personally,' says Steck. 'It really destroyed me. What happened there I still don't understand. We can discuss the situation up on the mountain, who was wrong, who was right. I can have my opinion and the Sherpas can have their opinion. But what was not okay was what happened in Camp 2. I totally lost trust in people. I'd never seen people like that. Even if it's another culture, it's not acceptable.

'In June, I just switched off,' he says. 'I already had Annapurna in my mind. I got into training. That was the easy escape. I never trained so hard in my life. It was hard when people were around. You could barely talk to me. The bad thing is that after Annapurna the whole thing came back.'

'Was it in your mind to do a solo ascent?'

'No. But you must understand that I can change my mind very quickly. I've been at the base of the Eiger north face with a guy, and he's said "I don't feel good", and I've said, "It's good weather, I'm going to climb for a bit." Because everything is right. I can go. It's possible. It's not like I never soloed before. I'll give it a try. I wasn't pissed off when Don turned around; I was just a bit frustrated. I thought I'd have a look. I wanted to use the two or three days of good weather.'

Steck says that if the ascent had been less spontaneous, he would have taken more care about recording it. 'But you still have to believe people,' he says. 'You can fake a lot if you want. If I had taken a picture at night you could doubt that; it could be anywhere. What if you take a GPS and the battery runs out 200 metres below the summit? Then people say you haven't done it. I made a GPS track on the Tre Cime. [Steck had recently climbed the Tre Cime's classic north faces in one day in winter with Michi Wohlleben.] Sometimes the track is completely weird. It shoots off in strange directions. The proof is never 100 per cent.'

'You're a professional climber. Don't your sponsors expect these things from you?' I ask.

'People have expectations of me, but sponsors don't.' When I express scepticism, he adds: 'They don't care. Really. They're happy. People now, they do all these commercial trips, shooting pictures during [sponsored] team trips. That's not what I want to do. I want to keep it focused and I want to keep it about climbing. That's how you push limits, not because my sponsor pays me.'

He also says he has turned down lucrative offers from outdoor companies to follow that path. I ask him about Tomaž Humar, another famous Himalayan solo climber who had a turbulent time from peers and media alike.

'I met him in 2005,' Steck says, 'when I climbed Cholatse north face. I had contact with him. I knew he was going to kill himself. That much was obvious. After Dhaulagiri he could not let go. After Annapurna, if I think I have to do something like that again, I'm going to kill myself. I have to find a completely different game.' He pauses. 'This whole business of the summit photos,' he says, a little bitterly. 'I think to myself, you assholes, I can show you, I can do another climb. I have these thoughts. But I think then I am dead.'

Why had he given such misleading answers to *Berner Zeitung*? 'I made a mistake with not checking carefully information I was using for my responses. My mistake. I cannot fact-check every interview. I cannot follow all the media.'

It doesn't seem an adequate response. There's nothing new in providing documentary evidence or, in its absence, a coherent account to support a claimed ascent, despite the – fraying – tradition in alpinism of taking a climber at his word. Reinhold Messner made certain to get a picture of himself on the summit of Everest during his solo ascent in 1980. The claims of Cesare Maestri on Cerro Torre and Tomo Česen on Lhotse's south face were fatally undermined by the sort of hazy description that prompted Steck's peers to ask questions.

Even so, Steck seems more confident than he had in recent interviews, largely because, a few days earlier, his cause had received an unexpected boost. Patricia Jolly of *Le Monde*, working on a book in Nepal about high-altitude porters, had taken the chance to interview Tenji Sherpa, one of Steck's team watching the mountain from advance base camp (ABC) on Annapurna. She also tracked down Nima Dawa, an assistant cook who remained at base camp, to his village in Solukhumbu. This interview took place without Jolly informing Steck. Both men said they saw Steck's headlamp high on the mountain, above the rock band, late on 8 October. 'At about 11.30 p.m. he was just below the summit,' Nima told Jolly, 'but I cannot estimate exactly how high. I woke up at 2 a.m. and I realised he had descended, seeing the light move down.'

Tenji, higher up the mountain at ABC, said he saw Steck's light about 200 metres below the summit at midnight. The Sherpas' timings roughly correlate with the account Steck gave Liz Hawley, unofficial record-keeper of climbs in Nepal since the 1960s. Hawley has since interviewed Tenji, who gave the same version of events.

Yet the Sherpas' statements begged several questions. Why did they wait months before going on the record, rather than mention this at base camp? Nima Dawa doesn't speak English, but Tenji does a little. And why didn't Don Bowie see anything on the mountain that night, when Tenji said he did? Why did they not speak of it in the morning? Why, according to Patitucci's blog, did Tenji say he only 'dreamed' Ueli reached the summit?

When I tracked him down, Tenji Sherpa said that he had indeed dreamed that Ueli Steck reached the summit, but not during the night of his climb. The dream occurred at base camp the night before. He recalled mentioning seeing Steck's headlamp to Bowie. Tenji said he did not see Dan Patitucci during his time outside his tent, and that he was unsure of precise timings. 'I got out of the tent at about 12 a.m. I came out just to see if I could see Ueli climbing. It must have been about 1 a.m. I saw him going up. He was about 150 metres or 200 metres below the summit.' Tenji's account differed somewhat from what he told Liz Hawley for her Himalayan database, but he also reiterated that he couldn't be certain of the exact time he noticed things.

Tenji said the summit of Annapurna isn't quite visible from ABC. 'There is a projection just beside the summit. That is where I saw him.' He said he saw Nima Dawa when they got back to base camp and they talked about the climb. That's when Tenji first heard that Nima Dawa had also seen the light from Steck's headlamp, and had seen it moving down at 2 a.m. (Nima Dawa, who spends the summer herding yaks, was out of contact and unable to confirm this.)

Don Bowie was adamant that you couldn't see a head torch from that distance, but I recalled my own experience high on a route in China. Friends and crew at base camp could see our head torches on our last bivouac eight or nine kilometres away and perhaps 1.8 kilometres higher. Steck was using a Tikka RXP, stronger than my torch, which also automatically varies the strength of its beam depending on where you look. The premise needs further testing but Tenji's evidence hasn't convinced Andreas Kubin. He argues that a Sherpa who suddenly pops up after four months saying he saw a light 'doesn't verify this ascent but doubles the doubt'.

Tenji comes from the remote village of Gudel, far from the more affluent region near Everest. He comes across as humble, almost apologetic. 'I only realised much later that there was a controversy regarding the climb when a French journalist called to ask me about it. Yes, Ueli climbed – we saw him go up. It is not because Ueli is a friend that I am saying he summited. Even Nima Dawa saw him.'

So far, evidence on both sides seems largely circumstantial. On one hand, the bizarre lack of GPS evidence and another camera mishap, on the other Steck's own – at times out-of-focus – testimony and that of the two Sherpas. If Tenji's and Nima Dawa's testimonies stand scrutiny, balance of opinion will probably shift to Steck.

Those who believe the fundamental values of alpinism have been drowned in a sea of commercialism would benefit from spending time with Yannick Graziani. When he says of climbing mountains, 'I'm doing these things for my reasons not anyone else's', you can believe him. Graziani's grandfather came from Corsica, hence the name, but he grew up just outside Nice, in a village called Tourettes-sur-Loup, not far from the Gorges du Loup, where he started climbing.

Over the last ten years or so, Graziani has featured in some remarkable Himalayan adventures, including the first ascent of the north ridge of Chomo Lonzo Central in 2005. Most of his climbs have been done as part of the TGW – with Christian Trommsdorff and Patrick Wagnon. He is the kind of climber who prefers to know his partners well and not discover their weaknesses on the mountain. 'I always do things step by step,' he says. 'My father told me when I became a father, now you have to be careful. I said to him, "Did you ever think I was not careful?"'

Graziani has known Stéphane Benoist since they were both boys rock climbing in the Maritime Alps, and after hearing the account of their ascent of roughly the same route Steck took on the south face of Annapurna, just a few weeks later, I couldn't help wondering if they wouldn't have survived had it not been for their friendship and understanding.

Steck left base camp almost immediately after his ascent, texting the two Frenchmen that he'd reached the summit. It didn't worry them. They'd been thinking of an alpine-style ascent of the Japanese pillar but they weren't sure of the route and Graziani had a hankering to do a line that went to the main summit, for aesthetic reasons more than anything else. 'We wanted to do our own way of climbing, in our own style,' he said.

Their ascent – begun a week later than Steck's and after half a metre of fresh snow had fallen – was very different and much slower, a point stressed by those who doubt the Swiss. The Frenchmen took a slightly different, safer line low down, bivouacked at 6,100 metres, and climbed the next day to a campsite at 6,650 metres that they knew about from their previous expedition. Here the weather worsened and, as Graziani puts it: 'You can't climb on Annapurna if there is one hour of snowfall because of spindrift.'

So, being well acclimatised, they holed up for three nights before continuing to the rock band, where Benoist led four very difficult pitches, up to M6. The névé and fat ice Steck says he used to climb fast had, apparently, been weathered off in the days that followed, but Benoist says he still found good ice above 7,000 metres. They had to rappel thirty metres to chop out a bivouac ledge at around 7,250 metres, wrapping themselves in the tent for a fitful night's sleep.

It didn't get much easier the following day. At 7,300 metres, Benoist found an old-style rigid Friend, one of those left by Lafaille and Béghin during their desperate retreat. Things have changed a great deal in the last twenty years. Graziani and Benoist, unlike their compatriots, had good weather forecasts and the confidence to move on – and they needed it. It would take two more camps, the highest at around 7,600 metres, before they were able to push for the summit early on the eighth morning. It was Graziani's fortieth birthday. 'You know, we felt good every night,' he says. 'The forecast was still good. We were well acclimatised and strong.'

But as they descended it became increasingly clear to Graziani that Benoist wasn't well. He was slow and didn't seem as sharp as he had been on the ascent. 'That night was terrible. The wind started to blow, a hundred kilometres per hour. We were still above the rock band. I was scared we would be trapped.' Neither of them knew that one of Benoist's lungs was slowly filling with fluid, not from pulmonary oedema but from an infection. Anxious for his partner's well-being, Graziani drove him on remorselessly next day, desperate to lose as much height as possible. 'I switched to survival mode,' he told me. 'I understood I had to take us down. It was a question of life and death.'

Having lost his headlamp, and with Benoist's out of power, Graziani resorted to using their stove as a light, as he rigged rappels deep into the night. 'I was worried I'd burn my jacket or drop the lighter.' At 3 a.m. they bivouacked at around 6,000 metres. By this point Benoist was suffering badly from frostbite, almost certainly a consequence of reduced lung function. Back in France, it would result in toes and some joints on his right hand being amputated.

Their story is both harrowing and uplifting, their achievement in some ways even greater than Steck's. Their partnership exemplified the spirit of the Piolets d'Or – and yet they had to settle for an honourable mention and a queue of journalists wanting to talk about Ueli Steck. 'Ten days after I came back from Annapurna, I met him,' Graziani said. 'We talked and talked.' He says they discussed the route in detail, and that Steck picked up his description and continued with it, and so they went on, 'each taking it in turns'.

'This made you confident that he had covered the ground?'

'Yes. As Stéphane says, it's a question of belief. Personally, I believe him.' Even so, Graziani says, 'Proof is important. It's a missed chance for him.' He went on to add: 'Ueli is very strong: mentally, physically, technically. To my mind he should have been sportsman of the year.'

Stéphane Benoist also believes Steck, although he says for different reasons than Graziani's. He is finishing lunch when I meet him, still adjusting to using a fork in a right hand ravaged by amputations, and awaiting to see if he will also need amputations on his left hand. Where Graziani is casual and direct, Benoist is thoughtful, almost professorial. It's his birthday, his forty-third; his wife is expecting their second child. Did he regret climbing Annapurna?

'No, I don't regret it. I mean, if I knew they were going to cut me like this then no, I wouldn't have gone. But now? No regrets.' Benoist is a guide, but hasn't been able to work since he got home, although he expects to return to the mountains in a year. In the meantime he has got by with help from clients and a public fundraiser in February in Chamonix. Steck attended and auctioned a signed ice axe. It sold for $9,000.

Benoist hadn't met Steck until they ate dinner together in Kathmandu before the expedition. He talks about how impressed he was with Steck's level of preparation, his experience at altitude and most of all his mental strength. 'It was clear to me that he was going to do something exceptional.'

Later, as we walked to Le Majestic to hear the various teams present their expeditions to the jury, he spoke again of Steck's psychology. 'You know, Messner was strong in the mountains and strong in the valley.' He meant that Messner was as forceful with the difficulties of his professional life, the demands of the media and the envy of his peers, as he was climbing Everest alone. 'Steck is just as strong in the mountains, but in the valley, perhaps not so.'

The next day, Ueli Steck was awarded a Piolet d'Or for his Annapurna climb, along with the Canadians Raphael Slawinski and Ian Welsted for their five-day ascent of K6 West in the Karakoram. In their frenzy to reach Steck, the European media largely overlooked Slawinski and Welsted. Steck told the *New York Times* that the sniping about his ascent was 'the downside of fame'.

In awarding Steck a prize, the jury inevitably brought attention to the criteria of the Piolets d'Or. George Lowe, one of the judges, told the *New York Times*: 'A bit more verification and emphasis on brotherhood of the rope would be my suggestions for improving the list of criteria.' The journalist Andreas Kubin was more forthright: 'Think about the rules and charter of the Piolets d'Or. Don't give prizes to the guys with the most innocent eyes, but to the one who is able to prove his achievement. This is the only way for the Piolets d'Or to keep its worth and for alpinism to keep credibility.'

Steck's prize has dragged a spotlight on to the true nature of modern alpinism and the role of sponsors and the media. Mountaineering is losing its lustre, under pressure from a media obsessed with risk and the commercialisation of Everest and the recent deaths of so many Sherpas there. How do you balance integrity and soul with the need to earn a living – and push the limits? Achievements like Steck's take time and training; that means money. Steck told Kubin: 'The fact is that I am the only one who knows that I summited Annapurna. It was a liberating experience. If someone wants to doubt it, they can. It is not for me to say how a climber has to prove his climb. It is for others to judge. So far, there have not been any official guidelines on how to document your successful ascent.'

For Kubin, the answer is clear: 'In the decade of GPS tracks, Handy-Cam and wristwatch computers one should be able to document [this kind of] achievement. And if you don't, you do a bad job as a profess-ional alpinist. In alpine history there will always be a big question mark on the solo ascent of Annapurna's south face – despite the Piolet d'Or.'

That's not a view shared by the British alpinist Jonathan Griffith, a friend of Steck's who has filmed him soloing in the Alps and was on Everest with him one spring. It's hardly surprising that Griffith is a supporter: 'As a photographer I get to see some of the world's best in action and I've never seen anyone move as fast and efficiently, and as confidently as Ueli.'

But it's the thought of regulating alpinism, of telling climbers what is and isn't acceptable that really disturbs him: 'Are we going to cross the line where every alpinist has to bring a special GPS tracker made for the exact purpose of "proof" on every climb that you do? By packing the box you're taking away a very important part of climbing – the pure independence and personal freedom and self-reliance that it offers. You are there for yourself; it is your line, your struggle.'

In the damp fog of controversy surrounding Ueli Steck there is one thing at least that supporters and sceptics – and even Steck himself – can agree on. Hansjörg Auer expressed it most forcibly. Having pronounced himself unimpressed with Steck's performance at the Piolets d'Or, he signed off: 'Whatever. He has to live with it … '

Ueli Steck died on 30 April 2017 on Nuptse while preparing to traverse Everest and Lhotse.

Lone Wolf

2014

It's easy to lose yourself in the hills around Verdon. The country is complex, and wild too, deep canyons and limestone peaks that freeze hard in winter but in summer are rich with the scent of thyme, lavender and pine. It didn't help that the road from Castellane to La Palud was closed for repairs. I followed detour signs until they petered out and then drifted along single-track roads coiling through forests past isolated farms. Pulling over to check the satnav I spotted some graffiti sprayed on a concrete bus stop. *Mort au loup*, it said. 'Death to the wolf.' Absent from France for much of the twentieth century, wolves are back, especially in remote corners of the Alps; farmers don't like it but city folk seem pleased by the idea. For them, commuting into work every day, it's exciting to think there's still an untamed world out there.

There was something wolfish about Patrick Edlinger. A photograph of him by Guy Martin-Ravel, one of the few from his zenith that the older Edlinger – puffy-eyed from cigarettes and alcohol – allowed on the walls of his house, catches this perfectly. His face is still narrow and long, framed by a shock of blond hair, his lips slightly pursed. The whole effect teeters dangerously toward the parody of a 1980s rock star – except for the eyes. Edlinger's gaze is fixed in the middle distance: intense, black – hungry.

You can see instantly what the whole of France could in the early 1980s, when Edlinger was one of the most famous men in the country. Aged just twenty-four, he appeared in the magazine *Paris Match* under the headline '*Les Français de l'Année*', photographed at the Paris opera house alongside actors Gérard Depardieu and Sophie Marceau; Hubert Curien, head of the European Space Agency; the songwriter Françoise Dorin and Laurent Fabius, the youngest prime minister in France's history.

The other men were in suits, but Edlinger wore cowboy boots, jeans and a loose, rustic leather jacket whose cut made it clear that Edlinger was, respectfully, not of their world and certainly not playing their games. *Paris Match* might have borrowed from Albert Camus and dubbed him the outsider, but the caption described him as an *alpiniste*. Edlinger was not really a mountain climber. True, he had done some impressive alpine routes in his late teens: the first winter ascent of the *Supercouloir* on Mont Blanc du Tacul and the north face of Les Droites. But he didn't care much for cold bivouacs or steep ice. He preferred the rough, sensuous touch of rock and the Provençal sun on his shoulders.

The French public had never seen anything like Patrick Edlinger before. Climbing to them was the heroism of Maurice Herzog on Annapurna, or the Alpine brilliance of Gaston Rébuffat, swinging in *étriers* on a granite face above Chamonix. Edlinger seemed wholly different, a child of nature, dressed only in shorts and emerging from the Verdon canyon as though born from the rock itself. Edlinger's climbing wasn't a symbol of anything, in the way Annapurna had been; it was a way of life, a state of mind.

'When I'm climbing rock,' he told *Actuel* magazine in 1981, 'it's like I'm talking to it. I'm courting it. There's respect in the way I use the holds. It's quiet; you're alone. No one needs anything from me, I don't ask anything of anyone. When you risk your life, your concentration has to be tenfold. You can't afford to make a mistake. There is no feeling like it. When you're on a big wall, you don't eat much. You're thirsty. It's horrible. You're going a long way, feeling like that. But when you're finished, that first taste of water, it stays with you for hours. It's important to keep life simple, because if your needs are great, you'll never be satisfied.'

For those sitting on the Métro, flicking through *Actuel* on the way home from work, it must have looked an enviable way to live, far from the daily grind, what the French call *le train-train quotidien*. Edlinger was the lone wolf living wild and free in the mountains. He compared climbing to yoga; he described himself as an ascetic. But those startling images of a beautiful young man high above the ground and his passionate explanation of a life lived on his own terms set him unknowingly on a course that would end thirty years later in tragedy.

Crossing the Pont de Soleils, I regained the road to La Palud, heading east to Point Sublime, below the village of Rougon. From here you get one of the best views of the Verdon Gorge; you look along it, your eye drawn to its immense depth, a crack in the planet whose rusty grey walls lean together over the spearmint river at its base. The campsites around La Palud were still closed for the winter and so were most of the *gîtes*, including L'Escalès on the edge of the village, the guesthouse Edlinger used to run with his wife, Matia. Walking in warm spring sunshine through the cobbled streets to the Bar de la Place, I bought a coffee, sitting outside at the table where Patrick had often stopped after a day's climbing.

You can't move through La Palud without being conscious of the impact climbing has had on this small village. Every other business has some angle to lure climbers in. Walking back to the car, I passed Le Perroquet Vert, a restaurant and *gîte* with a climbing store attached and a note outside with a phone number in case there are any out-of-season climbers in need of gear. You know you're in one of the world's premier climbing destinations.

It wasn't always like this. In the late 1960s, when climbing here got going, the village's population was half what it is now and in sharp decline. Climbing's free-climbing revolution played a big role in breathing new life into the place. Edlinger arrived in 1975 as a fifteen-year-old, part of a gang of climbers from Toulon dubbed La MJC. One of its stalwarts, Christian 'Kiki' Crespo, took him up *La Paroi Rouge*, recently climbed as an aid route with two bivouacs. Before they set out, Edlinger's mother warned Kiki that her son had the habit of sleepwalking; she'd once had to rouse him from the bathtub.

Kiki's tendency for late starts meant sleeping on the wall was inevitable, but with hundreds of metres of fresh air under his hammock, he made sure the boy was tied in securely and they topped out early next morning. The climb was a landmark for Patrick, and the start of a lifelong passion for the gorge; it seemed the perfect habitat for him. A year after his death, I felt his presence everywhere I went in Verdon. Edlinger may not have started the free-climbing revolution here, but he was its most famous ambassador. It's where he chose to live and work; it's where he married and where his daughter Nastia was born. Verdon is where he felt most free.

It would also become his prison.

Patrick Edlinger was born in Dax, a spa town in Aquitaine, south-west France. His father Jean-Marie was a pilot for the army, flying reconnaissance missions. His mother Éliane was from Barcelonnette, not far from the Italian border in Haute Provence. The town lies in the Ubaye valley, between three of France's most beautiful parks, the Écrins, the Mercantour and the Queyras. The landscape of his mother's family would have a strong impact on his imagination.

Patrick's maternal grandfather, Louis Bottero, was also, according to Jean-Michel Asselin's biography, a powerful influence, and friends like Catherine Destivelle could see the resemblance between them. An engineer and entrepreneur, Bottero invented a new kind of combined-harvester and adapted all kinds of machinery to work in the mountains; Patrick also loved machines, especially cars and motorbikes. Bottero was like Patrick a one-off, someone who could only live life on his own terms – and he was tough. Patrick often told the story of how Louis near-severed two fingers on a metal grinder and summoned the doctor to see if anything could be done. The doctor took one look and said the only option was hospital – and amputation. Instead Louis picked up some scissors and cut through the remaining flesh to finish the job.

The birth of their first child was not only meaningful to Jean-Marie and Éliane in the way it would be to anyone, it also prompted a shocking coincidence, one that would cause Jean-Marie to regard 15 June as his own rebirth. About to board his aircraft, news arrived that Éliane had gone into labour; Jean-Marie handed the mission to a friend and drove to hospital. Later, having held his infant son, he learned his replacement had crashed and died. Without Patrick, Jean-Marie would say, I wouldn't be here.

Days after Patrick was born, Éliane took the baby to live with her family in Barcelonnette, while Jean-Marie continued his service at different bases in France and in Algeria, where the French were on the verge of losing the war of independence. His father's regular absences were difficult; Patrick told Asselin of resenting the strange man holding his mother's hand when she met him at the school gate one day. So Jean-Marie took the chance of leaving the army to join a new customs surveillance unit, flying helicopters over the Mediterranean on the hunt for contraband. The family moved to La Seyne-sur-Mer, a suburb of Toulon, and Patrick enrolled at a local primary school.

Holidays were spent in the mountains. In winter, Patrick learned to ski and in the summer his parents took him and his sister Corinne camping, especially to Ailefroide in the Écrins. He joined the Éclaireurs Unionistes de France, a version of the Scouts. As a man he was lean and sinuous, like a dancer. As a boy he was, as the French say, *costaud* – beefy. But he relished the outdoor life, hiking in the hills, breathing the mountain air and learning to camp.

Inevitably there was climbing. Toulon is fringed with cliffs, the best of which is Baou de Quatre Ouro, rising to the north of the city where it catches the full force of the mistral. Many of the boy's first climbs were here, although Éliane did wonder if climbing was Patrick's thing after he burst into tears getting stuck on a route that was a little harder than usual. But the pleasure he took from their holidays at Ailefroide, and his fluid, easy movement on the boulders there, persuaded Jean-Marie that his son had talent.

When Patrick turned thirteen, Jean-Marie tried to get the boy into the French Alpine Club, but in those days there was an age limit. Casting around, he discovered the MJC, a more freewheeling bunch who spent weekends roaming the cliffs of southern France that was happy to take the teenager with them. Many of them had fathers working in the naval yards of Toulon, a blue-collar crowd, down-to-earth and self-reliant. After only two or three weekends, he was climbing routes in the 6s – E1/E2 and up – and carried on from there.

The contrast with his school life couldn't have been greater. Patrick's parents had chosen a Catholic school run by the Marist Brothers. Although the boy behaved well enough, he found schooldays tedious and spent his lessons with a climbing book open on his lap. He tore through the classics – Lionel Terray, Gaston Rébuffat – but his particular hero was Gary Hemming, the beatnik whose star had shone so brightly in the mid 1960s, the alpinist whose daring rescue of fellow climbers from the Dru had made the pages of *Paris Match*. Hemming seemed to embody everything that Patrick loved about climbing; it meant freedom, not a means to an end, but a way of being. It meant to be on the edge of things, to be the honest outlaw, living by your own rules. Patrick learned off by heart René Desmaison's judgement that Hemming 'ignored all boundaries and laws, loved life passionately without constraints of any kind'.

Unsurprisingly, his studies suffered. All he wanted was out. His future was in the mountains; why waste time at school? So his parents made him a deal. Graduate, and he'd get a small allowance that would allow him to climb and train full-time, with a view to becoming a mountain guide or ski instructor. Patrick could smell freedom and set to work, passing his *bac* to graduate from high school with one of the better marks in his class.

Finished with school aged sixteen, he grew his hair into the blond mane that became his hallmark. 'Le Blond' still spent his weekends at Verdon or Cimaï with his friends from the MJC and took his first trips abroad with them, flying to America for the first time, climbing Half Dome and the *Triple Direct* on El Capitan. But during the week, when his mates were at work, Patrick was forced to spend a lot of time climbing on his own. He'd make long traverses to build up stamina and cautiously worked his way through the grades at Baou. Sometimes he'd manage to pick up a partner for the day, but mostly not. Seeing his frustration, Robert Exertier, one of his friends from the Yosemite trip, told him about a climber of about his age from Nice, who was spending his days in much the same way and was similarly committed. His name was Patrick Berhault. 'He was,' Edlinger said of Berhault, 'the kind of man who makes you feel good inside. I haven't met too many like that.'

Across the Isère River from the university in Grenoble is a sleepy crescent of land called the Île d'Amour. Jean-Michel Asselin, one of France's best-known climbing writers and a former editor of *Vertical* magazine, moved here a few years ago and when I arrive is hard at work remodelling the house. Asselin knew Edlinger for thirty years, often ghosted articles for him and in the last months of Patrick's life was working with him on his life story.

'The two Patricks, they were like brothers,' Asselin tells me. For four years they shared the same goals, driven by the same intense ambition. Their bible was Reinhold Messner's *The Seventh Grade*. Their fervent prayer was to tear it up in the Alps and join the pantheon of heroes. Their ritual was a strict regime of training. When Edlinger discovered Berhault could trump his one-arm pull-up with a one-finger pull-up, he worked to go one better and do a pinky pull-up.

It's fair to say that of the two, Patrick Berhault was the more devoted. Patrick Edlinger had long had girlfriends, and getting up early to go for a run wasn't easy if you were leaving someone else's bed. Berhault avoided that complication in his life. He was more private, more focused. Perhaps it was an early indication of how their paths would eventually diverge.

Following the path of self-discipline allowed them to bend the petty rules of the material world. Climbing in Verdon, they'd squat in empty vacation homes and sleep rough in barns. They stole what they could, especially jars of Nutella, pretty much their staple diet. Berhault drove them around in a wheezy Peugeot, admitting to Edlinger that he didn't have a licence. In early 1980 their dreams of being mountaineering stars began to come true. The two made a string of impressive winter ascents in the Alps, including the *Supercouloir*, and a tough route on the northwest face of Ailefroide in the Massif des Écrins, the rugged and less frequented outlier of the Western Alps.

'But you know, Patrick Edlinger didn't like the cold,' Asselin says. 'He said it's not for me. Later, when they climb together again, he told Patrick Berhault, "On rock I'm okay, but the snow and ice, I don't do." It was clear between them.'

If their early ambitions were in the mountains, they actually became famous as leading activists in the sport-climbing revolution unfolding in France. Attention was turning away from the Alps to places like Verdon and Buoux, where free climbing was galloping ahead. Verdon in particular saw a radical change. The first routes had been done on aid ground up and followed crack lines between the soaring blank walls. Jacques Perrier changed all that with *Pichenibule*, a masterpiece of route finding equipped from above.

It was Patrick Berhault who, in 1980, freed *Pichenibule*, which even now is a notorious sandbag at 7b+. That November he climbed France's first 7c+, *La Haine*, on his home cliff of La Turbie above Monte Carlo. That same same year Patrick Edlinger on-sighted a 7b+, *La Polka des Ringards*, at Buoux. Their appetite for rock seemed insatiable. Edlinger climbed thirteen of Verdon's classic routes in a day, 2,500 metres of rock in a day, with Jacques Perrier seconding in tennis shoes because his feet were so sore. The two Patricks also became notorious for the bouts of soloing they did together. After all they'd faced in the Alps – the cold, loose rock, avalanches – it didn't seem that asinine to them.

'Soloing is such a personal thing,' he wrote in his journal when only seventeen or so. 'You always have that awareness that you might die, but please believe that I don't want to lose my life looking for some kind of glory. I want to enjoy this life of mine. Soloing is simply a way to go further in the regions of fear, to understand them better. Soloing is dangerous, but it's the best thing.'

The images this new free-climbing boom produced of beautiful young people pasted to shining white walls in dizzying situations were irresistible to the media. They filtered upwards, through the pages of climbing magazines and into publications like *Actuel*, where they attracted the attention of documentary filmmakers, among them Jean-Paul Janssen, who as a cameraman in Vietnam had filmed John McCain in captivity, and worked on a number of notable adventure film projects including the Robert Redford vehicle *Downhill Racer*.

Janssen could sense something in this climbing revolution and worked at first with several of its protagonists, including Perrier, Berhault and Edlinger, feeling his way to something grander. Berhault was as romantic and photogenic as Edlinger, but he was in no way a performer. Climbing for him was a precious mystery that lost something when it was dissected for public display. Edlinger was different. He could articulate why the life he was leading was so appealing. 'My way of life is travelling from crag to crag in my van,' he told Janssen. 'What I love is living in nature, the feeling of nature. I'm not pressured by life when I'm here. We're not mystics, I'm no different from anyone else. Climbing is my passion but it's also my job; I just happen to be better at it than most people. There are times when I'd rather be doing something else; more than training it's motivation that's key.'

The first film they made together, *La Vie au bout des Doigts*, 'living on your fingertips', was a sensation. Casting around for a good location, they tried first at La Piade, a sea cliff near Toulon, but it was a bust, and almost on a whim they headed to Buoux. While Janssen and his crew took in the beauty of the cliffs, Patrick warmed up with some solos. Janssen couldn't believe it. Would Edlinger do this with a camera on him? Patrick shrugged. Why not?

'This film changed Patrick's life totally,' Asselin says. 'It had an incredible impact. The public didn't know climbing. It was a secret. They might have seen people in Fontainebleau. They knew about Maurice Herzog and Annapurna. And now here was this guy, very beautiful, very elegant.'

The film's money shot was Edlinger hanging one handed from the overhang on the crux of the four-pitch 6a+ *La Béda*. Today, in the era of Alex Honnold, this doesn't seem a big deal, but in 1982 it was startling. Yet the film's fundamental appeal lay elsewhere, according to Asselin. 'The film's impact also came from what Edlinger says. It's the first time there is a guy like this who says what the meaning of climbing is, why he does it. How it's his life and not just a sport. How he doesn't need anything.'

A film that cost around $20,000 to make was sold by the French TV station Antenne 2 to twenty-five countries, generating revenues of $25 million. It won a hatful of prizes, and was nominated in 1984 for a César, the French equivalent to an Emmy. The advertising guru Jacques Séguéla, who worked on several French presidential campaigns, said Edlinger's image as a *primitif* in an increasingly artificial world was a banker. Janssen told Patrick to keep a copy of *La Vie* close at hand: 'In thirty years you'll be able to show it and it will still earn for you.'

With cash from new sponsorship deals, Edlinger upgraded his mobile home and found himself in Paris, the regular guy from Toulon swept up in a glittering social world. Entertainers in particular seemed to respond to him. He was at singer Serge Gainsbourg's house and hung out with the maverick comedian Coluche. Imagine Ron Kauk chilling with Bob Dylan and John Belushi and you'll get the idea. There were plenty of drugs, although Edlinger steered clear, and plenty of women eager to meet him, which was a lot more congenial.

The impact *La Vie* had on climbing in France was profound. It was like a bomb going off; nothing was ever the same. Young boys crowded into the sport, and young women too, eager to catch the wave. The French climber Arnaud Petit said in the mid 1990s that eighty per cent of those, including himself, climbing in France did so because of *La Vie*. 'I was eleven when I saw *La Vie*, climbing in my own little world in Albertville. There was no culture of climbing. That film was galvanising.' Because soloing had been such a large part of the first film, in Janssen's follow-up, *Opéra Vertical*, Edlinger was eager to show those young people that climbing really meant using ropes and being with another person, that he wasn't simply the lone Spartan doing something crazily dangerous.

How the climbing world itself felt about Edlinger's sudden rise to international fame was more complex. Most French people thought he was the best climber in the world, but by the mid 1980s, a group of Parisian climbers, notably Antoine and Marc Le Menestrel and Jean-Baptiste Tribout, were pushing past Edlinger, climbing routes of 8a and beyond. In 1984, British climber Jerry Moffatt arrived at Verdon and quickly despatched an open project Edlinger had bolted called *Papy On Sight* at 7c+. Some pointed out that it was Patrick Berhault who was the true star from the south, but Edlinger who was reaping the rewards from big sponsorship deals. 'He got a lot of money,' Asselin says, 'but not as much as people think. He turned down a lot of publicity deals as well. His mother did his accounts; that stuff didn't interest him. He was not so good in business. He had an agent who created a big problem with Japanese TV that ended in the courts.' From the outside it looked different, creating resentment, even jealousy.

There was something backwards about Patrick Edlinger's career. Nationally famous in his early twenties, his best climbing achievements came later. But in the meantime he had to cope with managing the expectations and pitfalls of his new situation. Even before *La Vie* was released, he and Patrick Berhault were following different paths. Berhault spun off into a series of experimental new directions. He climbed the *American Direct* on the Dru with Jean-Marc Boivin and then flew by hang-glider to climb the south face of the Fou. He created a kind of vertical dance as an art project, set up climbing youth schemes in the suburbs of Lyon and even settled down for a spell as a farmer and carpenter in the Massif Central.

What Berhault didn't do was participate in climbing competitions. Not only was he one of nineteen signatories to a public manifesto opposing them, he was pretty much the only one who stuck to the principle. Patrick Edlinger did not sign but was away climbing in the United States when the first official competition was held, at Bardonecchia in the summer of 1985. He was in Europe the following year and won the event.

In Edlinger's relatively short competition career, the unquestionable highlight was his victory at Snowbird in 1988. The event may have been a financial train wreck, but as a piece of theatre it could not have been bettered. The backstory was Edlinger's recent repeat of Jibé Tribout's Verdon route *Les Spécialistes*. Tribout had graded it 8c; Edlinger took it down a peg to 8b+. This act of arrogance from someone thought to be off the pace was insufferable. Tribout wanted to know on what basis he felt able to judge his route? The tension between Edlinger and those Johnny Dawes once called 'the poshies from Paris' was near its height.

Last to climb, Edlinger flowed past the high point of each of his competitors, Tribout included. Spectators, sensing they were in the presence of something exceptional, found themselves transfixed. Edlinger paused below the final overhang that so far no one had overcome, the tension building. At that moment, a narrow shaft of sunlight pierced the cloud cover to illuminate Edlinger pulling through in his moment of triumph, as though the very heavens had anointed his talent.

His win at Snowbird was glorious but the grind of competitive climbing began to take its toll. Before, he had competed without a care in the world; now he was expected to win. Competing at Nîmes in the inaugural World Cup, Edlinger was kept in isolation for twelve hours before his qualifying round, read the start of the route wrong and slipped off the first move. 'I had never been a competitive animal and this ridiculous failure confirmed my suspicion that these artificial walls weren't for me.' And that was that.

For Edlinger – restless, passionate – exploring the world and being in nature was part of the deal. So he swapped the glare of the spotlight for a feast of new routing. The prompt came from the old blacksmith at Buoux who had retired through ill health and was now living in a village on the edge of the Écrins. Edlinger, a friend, went to visit him before taking a long trip to America. Above the blacksmith's home was a mountain called Céüse. 'When I saw the cliffs,' he recalled, 'I tore up my plane ticket. I spent the next four years there.'

The late 1980s were Edlinger's best years as a climber. There were the new routes at Céüse and his solo of the 8a *Orange Mécanique* at Cimaï. After repeating *Les Spécialistes* and winning at Snowbird, he repeated Ben Moon's fierce new routes *Agincourt* at Buoux and *Maginot Line* at Volx, both 8cs and both contenders for being the world's hardest. On *Maginot Line* Edlinger even figured out an elegant new sequence that took the grade down a notch. Yet by the early 1990s the climbing revolution he had heralded was gently ushering him off the stage.

He remained in formidable shape. British climber Stevie Haston, no slouch himself when it came to training, climbed a lot with Edlinger in the early 1990s. 'I really liked him. He was a great guy. He was solid and had an immaculate technique. For me, he was the best of that era.' Patrick showed Haston the routes at Cimaï and then they'd go home to his training room and work out. 'We'd do ten, twelve-hour days.' They spent months together at Hueco Tanks, during his bouldering phase. 'I remember doing problems with Patrick and Skip Guerin – two of the earliest and two of the best.'

Some climbers in his position might have found a graceful way to let go, but Edlinger was too much invested in his own story to close the book for good, and he needed the money. The magazine features and climbing trips continued; he remained on television and in films and advertisements. 'It got harder and everyone else got better,' Haston says. Yet while there was a creeping sense of nostalgia in these projects – in 1998 he appeared in the movie *Verdon Forever* – it's difficult to see quite when and how his life fell apart so badly.

Some suggested a near-fatal accident he suffered in 1995 might have prompted his decline. An inattentive belayer, a broken hold and Patrick hit the ground from twelve metres up, curled into a ball that bounced a metre in the air. His heart stopped, but one of his companions had the skills to resuscitate him. In the helicopter on the way to hospital, unable to move, he told Jean-Michel Asselin that he contemplated ways to kill himself if he really was paralysed. 'If I was going to be a vegetable, how would I do it?' Life without movement would be unthinkable. But he hadn't broken a bone; his muscles were simply all in spasm and he was soon back climbing again.

In 2004, while on an epic climbing traverse of the Alps, attempting all eighty-two peaks over 4,000 metres in just eighty-two days, Patrick Berhault stepped unroped through a cornice near the summit of the Täschhorn and fell 600 metres. 'Berhault's death had a big impact,' Asselin says. 'It was me who called Patrick, who was in Italy. I said I had bad news. He said: "Is it Patrick?" I told him it was, that he'd been in a fall. He said: "Ah, *le cons*. The idiot." He cried out, and then he said that we had to go at once and find him. I said: "No, Patrick, it's not possible." Later he called me back and said that he knew Patrick was dead and that we couldn't do anything. It was very hard for him. From then on, Patrick thought about him every day.'

There had been rumours the two Patricks had fallen out before Berhault's death and *Actuel* ran a feature suggesting it was true, wondering what had happened to the heroes it had featured in the early 1980s. The suggestion, Asselin says, enraged Edlinger. 'There were no arguments. They just had different goals. They followed what each other did and when Berhault called Patrick with an idea to climb in the Alps, he said yes without asking what it was. They were as they had always been.'

There is footage of the two of them in this era, at the start of the 2000s, when they climbed hard routes in the Dolomites, like *The Fish* on the Marmolada; it's moving to see these childhood friends reunited, still climbing hard and in love with it. Edlinger was now living in Verdon with his new wife, Matia, who ran the *gîte* he bought. The birth of their daughter Nastia in 2002 – and how Patrick felt about that – is captured in a beautiful photograph of the three them together. He even foreswore soloing as too irresponsible for a new father.

But the marriage soured, and his sense of the walls closing in around him intensified. He dropped from view and began drinking hard. After Berhault's death his passion for climbing faded. Verdon was no longer his playground; it became his prison. 'Patrick was very clear about his depression,' Asselin says. 'It came on after his marriage. Alcohol was the solution to the problem, to feel a little more human. But of course it made things worse. Finally, when they separated, he was alone in the Verdon.'

Catherine Destivelle was his close contemporary and with a similar media profile. Both starred at Snowbird. She recalls meeting him with the film-maker Gilles Chappaz. 'What makes me sad is knowing that at the end of his life perhaps not enough was done to help. But it was difficult, he isolated himself. Patrick was telling me he was going to do the hardest climbs in the world and do a book. He said he was back climbing but I knew he wasn't. He couldn't accept that he was less strong. When he died, and it was in the news, my son asked who was Patrick Edlinger?'

Asselin plays me his final interview with Edlinger, made ten days or so before his death. It is harrowing to hear. Edlinger articulates his desperate journey through depression and alcoholism, how he lost confidence in himself, how he made mistakes and the terrible loneliness he endured. 'People don't want to see you and you don't want to see them,' he says. At times he is defiant and proud: 'I don't give a damn what people think.' Then he says sadly that he can count his true friends on the fingers of one hand. When he says that he has spent years in hell, you don't need to see his ravaged face to believe him.

Towards the end, he had bouts of renewed optimism. He told Asselin he was going to take on the world again. 'He would say: "I am Patrick Edlinger. I can climb 9a, 9b." I said: "That's true, you are Patrick Edlinger. But Edlinger today is not the same. That one has gone."'

His parents were living nearby and over the years kept an eye on him. He'd also begun a new relationship with Anne-Christine Gimenez, a sailor who lived and worked on the remote island of La Réunion, where she kept her yacht. In the book he and Asselin worked on together, Edlinger credits her for helping him escape the darkest period of his life. His time with her would lift him out of his depression but he suffered when he finally had to fly home. 'Sometimes I think that if he'd seen the book, or finished the film with Gilles, that it might have helped,' Asselin says. 'I think also that by saying publicly he was in this terrible situation he thought he would get out of it. But I understood very well that he was not getting out.'

Patrick died on 16 November 2012. Four days earlier he and Asselin spoke for the last time. Patrick was due to appear in Grenoble, at a special screening of *La Vie*. 'He said he didn't want to come, that he wasn't well. I tried to convince him, said that people wanted to see him. His father tried to convince him. I asked him what he was afraid of, whether it was seeing people, or people seeing him? He'd changed a lot since those films came out. But it wasn't really that. He was afraid of what he thought about himself. He felt embarrassed for himself.'

It was Jean-Marie who discovered his son's body. He and Éliane were silent afterwards, prompting speculation that Patrick had committed suicide, but they were simply too heartbroken to speak. The reality was a moment of carelessness, a banal accident. Jean-Marie had found Patrick on the floor of his bathroom with a head injury. He had fallen from a flight of steps, not for the first time, and crawled back up them to wash the wound, before collapsing. He was fifty-two.

Younger climbers who had grown up when Patrick was at his height paid tribute to the impact he had on their lives. Liv Sansoz, a two-time world champion, said: 'He was an enormous inspiration to climbers, including me. You saw all the pictures; he was the god of his era, a myth. He motivated me. The first time I met him – that was a super day. I climbed with him, we tried the same route; we shared experiences. He was the true pioneer in spreading the word about climbing to the general public, as well as pushing the sport at the top level. He broke barriers.'

Many of the climbers and friends who had lost touch over the years were at the ceremony marking his life. The French sports minister Valérie Fourneyron spoke of her shock at his early death, and the affection the French people felt towards him. 'Patrick was an icon,' Asselin says finally. 'I was surprised at the showing of *La Vie* in Grenoble. A lot of young people there had never seen the film and they liked it. He represents something. He was something important.'

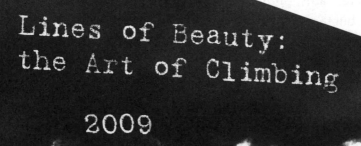

Lines of Beauty:
the Art of Climbing

2009

Driving out of Les Praz towards Chamonix, I catch sight of an old man in my rear-view mirror walking stiffly along the opposite side of the road, hoisting his left leg in the air to move forward. I register the iron-hard Aiguilles looming over him and look ahead again. A heartbeat later, I realise I know this man. He is not some anonymous pensioner, but Andy Parkin, one of the best alpinists Britain has ever produced and a successful full-time artist. We are going to the same place, he and I, the gallery in Chamonix that exhibits his work. In fact, I've spent the afternoon tracking Parkin down. So I pull over and wait.

Two questioning blue eyes appear at the open door. A mane of blond hair, dirtying to gray, falls forward a little as he leans down. It's an experienced, sharp-nosed face, but not an old one. His jacket is a little ragged. His scarred left hand rests on the door frame as he scans the interior of the preternaturally clean rental car, like an animal sniffing a new cage, and then levers himself into the passenger seat.

It's fair to say he's not wildly pleased to see me. In summer, when climbers and tourists choke the valley, Parkin tends to retreat a little, hunkering down in his stamp-sized apartment and his studio, patiently following the ascetic path he chose for himself two decades ago: climbing and creating without compromising his carefully thought-out vision. Interruptions by visiting climbers are a distraction. In the winter he is planning to return to Tierra del Fuego and he has a lot of work and preparation to get through first. He's just completed filming for a documentary about his life. He's had enough of talking about the past.

'I'm not normally in the front line trying to explain,' he says. 'Trying to impress people. Why should they care? It's way too personal for all that. There are enough people out there in climbing who want to talk. Let them. The climbing's for me. I don't care what people think. My friends, people I respect, I'd rather have their respect than not, but, y'know … ' And he trails off. Talking about his life also requires him to revisit the accident that nearly killed him in 1984, leaving him with injuries that would qualify him for a disabled parking permit, should he ever buy a car. It's an old story, and one that Parkin is done with.

His art is a different matter. He's going to the gallery now for its regular Wednesday evening open house, organised by owner Johnny Reid. We chat and drink wine. Parkin talks more freely now, as if he's adjusted to the idea of my being here. We arrange to go climbing the next day. People start arriving. An elderly couple drags Parkin away to explain a painting. As I leave, I catch sight of their faces turned towards his, their attention rapt. His hands are pulling shapes from the air. In the warmth of the room, his shirt is open a little at the neck, his face a little pinker – an unselfconscious display of passion. It's hard to believe I'd mistaken him earlier for an old man. Parkin now shines with the intensity of someone half his age.

It's that intensity that I've travelled to Chamonix to find. Because while Parkin's climbing is important, at least tangentially, to what I'm trying to find out, it's his artist's way of seeing that seems most essential. I can't think of many climbers who have put more thought into what it means to be an alpinist than he has, or applied such a creative imagination to the task of climbing difficult routes. That's what I want to capture, the art of climbing, the spark of creativity, the shift in perspective that changes the way you – and others – view the world.

Why now? I don't honestly know. Maybe it's my time of life putting all these questions and doubts in my head about climbing and what it means to me. What it's *for*. Twenty-five years ago, almost to the day, I first came to this valley as an overgrown boy, wearing ill-fitting boots that gave me blisters and an old rugby shirt that soaked up sweat as I laboured under a borrowed pack in the August heat. Chamonix seemed like an existential kindergarten. Here was a place I could find out who I was, invent myself – write myself a story. Unwashed and awkward in our filthy T-shirts, with our faces crisped by the sun at altitude, my teenage friends and I gorged on patisseries (but only after we'd done a route, not before). Beautiful girls turned their heads away as they passed us on the town's main street. At that age, it still seems possible to grow up into the ideal version of yourself who stars in your daydreams. The version where the beautiful girls didn't turn their heads away.

One season, I dossed in an abandoned trailer. Another year, I camped in the woods behind a parking lot on the edge of town. The site was popular with flat-broke Eastern European climbers and their strange, home-made gear. We'd sit around the campfire sharing beers as they sang their songs. One morning I woke at dawn to see a man prowling through the trees, his arms describing arcs through the dew-heavy air. He was from northern California, which to me seemed as distant and wondrous as Mars. I nudged the bloke sleeping next to me, and pointed at the strange vision. Any amazing thing, it seemed, could happen in this place.

'Tai chi,' he mumbled. 'He's doing tai chi. Chinese martial thingy. Now fuck off and let me sleep.'

This was in 1986, the year of what became known in London's financial district as the 'Big Bang,' essentially the starting gun for the turbo-powered capitalism that would transform Chamonix, along with the rest of the world. The trailer is long gone. Camping in the woods is now forbidden. The tai-chi man is probably twice divorced in LA, working at some banal job and failing to meet his child-support payments. The last time I climbed in Chamonix, a couple of years ago, I slept in a comfortable bed, in the chalet of a wealthy friend. I ate in restaurants and talked about the price of property. I walked straight past the patisseries. These days, I'm trying to cut back on cholesterol.

What had happened to that naive sense of possibility? Did I just get older? Or had I got it wrong? Had I wasted the last few years climbing through habit, trying to recreate some youthful enthusiasm, just because I couldn't think of anything else to do? Was I reading too much into an activity that had shaped my life because, having invested so much in it, I needed it to be true? I could have done something more useful, or made money and bought my own damn chalet. I couldn't help feeling I liked the kid living in the trailer more than who he'd become.

Andy Parkin still hangs on in his little apartment, a tenacious survivor of Chamonix's bohemian past. But since he moved here in 1983, consumerism has grown like a fungus throughout the climbing world, spreading deep underground among the roots of our activities, fed by the compost of financial interest. The emphasis on sponsorship and earning power becomes heavier with each passing year. With that change has come a need to differentiate between climbers. Overt competition and rankings are the business of sport: you're not necessarily trying to be original; you're trying to be better than the next guy. Climbers, and the industry that supports them, have come to emphasise grade, height and speed, all things that can be measured.

Imagination, creativity and thoughtfulness, the unquantifiable, have faded from view. I felt – feel – that these qualities ought to be part of mountaineering, or else the pursuit would be diminished. So should a feeling for the mountains, a sense of place, an attentiveness to the world outside your own story. Somewhere other. Maybe talking to Parkin would help me see all that clearly again.

'The *how* is so important in climbing,' Parkin tells me, drinking tea outside his studio the next day. 'It's the reason we do it. It's gratifying to be successful, to have ambitions and all that. But the actual execution has got to be as pure ethically as I can make it. Otherwise there's no point. I'd rather not go near it. I don't ever want to become complacent about anything. For fear of losing that edge. The creative edge, not the sporting one.'

'I know a lot of climbers who don't necessarily love the mountains,' he continues. 'They love the activity, they love the sport. But it's not the same love of someone who *really* loves the mountains, every aspect from the moraine, from the brooks or streams at the bottom. Their moods.'

Parkin and I both grew up in Sheffield, the original steel town. We learned to climb on gritstone crags up on the moors above the city's western fringe. Unlike Parkin, I came back to Sheffield to bring up our family and reconnect with a landscape that is, for better or worse, the place where I feel most at home. But this is the same visual world that underpinned Parkin's childhood, a critical influence in the making of an artist. And plenty of other mountain artists remain here.

Unlike Chamonix, the last quarter century hasn't been so generous to Sheffield's fortunes. That's good news for artists looking for cheap rents. A month before my trip to see Parkin, I found Jim Curran surrounded by large canvases, finished and unfinished, in a former commercial property turned studio space.[1] 'As I get older,' he said, sorting through some brushes, 'the crags get smaller and the paintings get bigger.' Once better known as a writer – *K2, Triumph and Tragedy*, his account of the mountain's disastrous 1986 season, is a classic of mountain literature – Curran also has fifteen films to his credit. But his first passion was painting. Now in late middle age he has taken it up again, producing a sequence of almost architectural pictures, often in vibrant colours, of the mountains and cliffs he had experienced first-hand. They have a presence about them, an expansive energy;

1. Author's note: Curran died in April 2016.

the cliffs seem to hum with life.

'I remember Al Alvarez once saying that these are the paintings of a climber, because you can see the routes on them. You've got an insight into the climber's reality, which tends to be cracks and overhangs and holds and so on,' explained Curran. 'A non-climber may not have that kind of insight. But I want my paintings to be viewed as paintings. Once you fall back on the "I'm a climber" sketch then you're only appealing to other climbers, and it becomes very introverted.'

Transfixed by physical perfection and performance, modern climbing photographers are prone to that kind of self-focus. Taking the experience for granted, they forget that it doesn't have to be the same for each. Facial expressions get blanker as sponsor logos get bigger. Software and lighting serve to exaggerate; they turn flesh-and-blood climbers into plastic action figures.

With the development of digital photography, manipulation means we're even less sure what we're looking at ever existed. In a way, it's part of a general speeding up and abstraction of our lives. Curran quoted David Hockney's view that it's hard to take an art like photography seriously when it only lasts one-sixtieth of a second. The turnover of information in the climbing world, as everywhere, keeps getting faster: from expedition websites to blogs to Twitter feeds. Everything becomes condensed, exaggerated, hyper-mediated.

The temptation to focus only on the instantaneous extreme – the most dramatic, the most beautiful or the most frightening – ignores all the textures and nuances of the climbing life. How rock looks and feels, how a mind can change after weeks in the mountains. A compulsion for the extreme ends up being oddly superficial, an adventure pornography that barely holds your attention.

Some climbers, maybe only a few, are still searching for an understanding of our world that breaks through its shiny, commercial surface. They have taken Hockney's hint, and gone back to a more rigorous, more considered artistic exploration. 'I think it's no coincidence that a load of mountain artists are emerging,' Curran told me. 'They're trying to do something more.' Something that climbing photography, often staged and usually designed for immediate sale, can no longer manage.

When we spoke, Curran mentioned the Cumbrian artist Julian Heaton Cooper, who comes from a Lake District dynasty of artists, grandson of the post-impressionist Alfred Heaton Cooper, and son of the water-colourist William Heaton Cooper. When Julian left Goldsmith's College of Art in the late 1960s he thought there was something 'anachronistic' about painting mountains. He wasn't convinced by the existing tradition of mountain art, a product of Romanticism, which spoke more to the psychological view of the time, that mountains were the geography of the unconscious rather than actual, physical places whose reality had to be respected. As a climber, however, Cooper found he couldn't leave mountains alone. Slowly, over decades, they re-emerged in his art.

Like Parkin, Cooper has been on artistic forays into the high mountains, sitting on glacial moraine, the canvas bull-clipped to a portable stretcher. He would leave the canvas on the mountainside at night. Often wind would blow grit and dust into the paint that became part of the picture. Over a decade, Cooper made a series of journeys, including treks to Kang-chenjunga and Kailash, which have produced some astonishing paintings. These are hardly landscapes in the traditional sense, but cropped elements that capture in realistic detail the fluted snow on Kangchenjunga's north face, or the golden smoothness of Kailash's walls. 'He approaches Kailash with such incredible focus and intensity that I'm surprised the Buddhists let him do it,' Curran joked. You feel, looking at these giant canvases, that only a mountain climber could have painted them.

What is it, in fact, that the climber brings to light? We're used to sports-people showing us what they are through their performances. How Johan Cruyff kicked a football, or Lynn Hill moves up rock. 'If you take Joe Brown and Don Whillans,' Curran told me, 'their routes are such an expression of their personalities. A Brown route is almost always subtle, understated, devious. *Vector* at Tremadog is the prime example of a brilliant solution to a complex problem. Whereas Whillans would start at the bottom and go straight to the top.'

But is there an art in climbing that's accessible to the rest of us mere mortals? All those years ago in Chamonix, climbing put my own mind in a state of continuous present, the Buddhist's 'be here, now' – the condition psychologists call 'flow'. Where was the creation that came out of that? Perhaps in the lines traced on photographs of cliffs I had climbed, or the shards of memory I carried forward, the stories I told. Before Curran got back to his painting he said to me, 'It sounds awful if you say that a Joe Brown route is a piece of sculpture, but in a sense it is.' Then he pauses. 'Johnny Dawes is another brilliant example.'

Dawes was one of the great British rock climbers in the 1980s and 1990s, a period of rapid growth in terms of difficulty but also imagination. As it happens we were at the same boarding school and through meeting him I became absorbed by climbing. His mind was just so not like everybody else's, stretching far beyond the concerns of our contemporaries – career, prospects and so forth. For a start, he seemed to imagine the world spatially, rather than verbally. That people couldn't share the shapes inside his head would leave him mute with frustration. At school, climbing on buildings, he did things I could not understand, that I knew even in my near ignorance were special.

Being shorter than average, Dawes, like the dimunitive Lynn Hill, sometimes had to make moves others could skip past, or else he had to use holds in a different way. It wasn't just that he expressed himself through climbing, fluidly, dynamically, even outrageously so – he created shapes you wouldn't ordinarily see, moving in a way that was entirely unexpected. That visual imagination for movement is more commonly the medium of the dancer, but in climbing, the choreographer is the rock.

As a boy, Dawes would fill his schoolbooks with naive drawings imitating Picasso's cubist period alongside lists of routes he wanted to climb. He'd sketch how the holds related to each other. He was on a quest to find the rock that would allow him to articulate the moves he saw in his head. Now you can go to certain cliffs and see those creations, like paintings in a gallery. Not only that, you can try to climb them and appreciate first hand their creator's talent.

Movement as art, in the way Dawes pursued it, and described it, is like an abstract painting brought to life. But that process has also worked the other way around. For a while, the 1960s British abstract artist Jeremy Moon had an ambition to become a choreographer, so he learned to dance. According to art historian Janet McKenzie, he 'took six months of intensive ballet classes, five nights a week'. Any ex-dancer will tell you that the physical demands this implies, particularly for a man already in his thirties, is a far more gruelling existence than most rock climbers experience. 'Choreography,' McKenzie concluded, 'subsequently informed his visual art, infusing it with a particular conception of movement, balance and harmony.'

Moon died in a motorcycle accident in 1973 at age thirty-nine. In the late 1980s, his son, Ben Moon, became one of the world's leading sport climbers and boulderers. Jeremy's urge to dance reappeared in the abstract patterns Ben found on blank pieces of stone. One art critic described a work by Jeremy Moon as 'a painting reminiscent of a frozen scene from some strange, symbolic mechanical ballet'. After reading that, you might find a photograph of Ben Moon on one of his landmark boulder problems seems different. Greater, maybe.

'Climbing is certainly more than just numbers and grades, which, when one first starts climbing, are totally meaningless,' Ben Moon tells me. He's drinking a strong espresso at his home in Sheffield, just round the corner from mine. 'I have always thought that it's the movement that draws you in and gets you hooked. This movement is more intense the closer you get to your limit, whatever that might be, perhaps because it's been so rehearsed. I suppose it's a bit like a dance. The physicality of climbing combined with these rehearsed movements is pretty addictive.'

'The rock is certainly more than just a stadium, which is why we are always searching for that one really special climb,' Moon continues. 'Perfect rock, perfect shapes, perfect moves. I couldn't really say what it's like to create a work of art, and although the experience of doing a hard first ascent or repeat can be quite some journey I am not sure if they would be the same. One thing my father did believe was that it took a lot of hard work and discipline to be a good artist and you had to work at it constantly even when you weren't motivated or feeling inspired, a bit like if you want to be a good climber.'

Another artist, Dan Shipsides, a lecturer at Ulster University, tried to bring the idea of rock climbs as sculptures into the Castlefield Gallery in Manchester. 'I designed the installation [Hanging Slabs] based on physical aspects of certain climbs,' he said. 'I was particularly keen to emulate a move on *Valkyrie*, where you're delicately moving on steep slabs, then step over an airy gap and shuffle round a hanging arête. It's very spatial. A beautiful moment, hanging in an airy precarious space.' Members of the public, non-climbers, were invited to have a go and bring a static abstraction to life, what Yoko Ono might have called 'a happening'. For Shipsides, it's not enough to look at landscapes; they have to be experienced.

Of course, you can just go climbing and have an event for yourself without needing to visit a gallery. But art teaches us how to comprehend our experiences, how to place them within the meaningful and provocative order of a composition. It's a vision so well communicated that we feel moved and involved in its energy. Richard Long, the only artist to be nominated for the prestigious Turner prize four times, winning it in 1989, has taken hiking as an art form, using photographs, text and maps to recreate a journey. Long's contemporary Hamish Fulton has extended that process even farther, to the summit plateau of Cho Oyu. When Fulton had a retrospective at Tate Britain in 2002, the critic Jonathan Jones wrote: 'Just in case you start savouring the classic beauty of his photographs of Himalayan boulders and American riverbeds, or appreciating the graphic ingenuity of his wall paintings, be advised that none of this is the core of the art, which is the walking – what you see is evidence that his art happened, that he walked from A to B. What makes the repetitiveness, dryness, silence of this exhibition so triumphant is not some chic pleasure in nothingness but something more difficult to accept and impossible to let go. Fulton's art is a goad.'

Like Long and Fulton, Parkin calls attention to the transitory line traced by a transitory human – something like those fleeting, essential moments that I'd felt in Chamonix. 'I wait for the conditions to draw a thin white line. And I love that contrast between the dark granite and the white ice. It's ephemeral and I love that.' He went to the Khumbu for the first time in winter 2008, climbing a new route alone on the north-east face of Phari Lapcha (5,977 metres) above the village of Gokyo, enduring bitter cold and coping with horribly loose rock near the summit. Before he started, he followed his usual pattern, wandering round the base of the peak, painting, tracing the line through his binoculars. He examined that line with decades of experience, as a climber, but also as an artist.

Look again at a topo for a big wall. Diagrammatic, practical, illustrative – topos can be all those things. But a topo is not just a guide, or even a goad. Is a topo evidence that art happened? Andy Kirkpatrick opens his book *Psychovertical* with a topo of El Capitan's *Reticent Wall*, the climb that dominates the narrative. Looking at the topo before and after reading his account is an altered experience, just as is rereading the guidebook description of a route that's stretched you. Before a route, you cross-examine a topo or a description for critical clues that will lead to success, or even survival. Afterward, they're changed into the paraphernalia of memory, like scars on your hands, or scratches on an ice axe. It intrigues me that Andy Kirkpatrick went to art school before he began climbing. Likewise, the architect Victor Saunders, in the process of dreaming up one of the landmark Himalayan ascents of the post-war period – the Golden Pillar of Spantik – drew the climb first, to imagine it better.

That such different characters – Parkin, Saunders, Dawes, Moon, Kirkpatrick – reach for a similar process in conceiving their climbs is more than a sportsman's trick of visualising success. In the intense way artists have of looking, their steady, fierce gaze, lies something grander, less utilitarian, more powerful, elusive and indefinable. It's what I saw in Parkin's face at the open door of my rental car. Here was a man who looks hard, as well as climbs hard.

The day after the gallery showing, Parkin and I drive up the valley and park under a pleasant south-facing crag about forty minutes from the road. We're here because it's convenient and not too serious. This is the kind of climbing I've probably done too much of in the last few years, bolt-protected and agreeable, full of good moves but oddly forgettable. The alpine climbs of my twenties and early thirties seared through me, branding memories like burning coals. It's been more challenging in recent years to find that keen, sharp heat. Maybe my brain has altered with age. Maybe I just have to accept I can't now force myself through that depth of experience.

Ironically, it was on this milder sort of cliff, on the Riffelhorn above Zermatt, that Parkin had his near-fatal accident over two decades ago. Lowering a client on the rope, his belay failed, and he fell ten metres on to his left side. At first, Parkin thought he'd cracked a few ribs, and half-expected to get up and shake it off. But his heart had been knocked out of its pericardial sack. People who suffer this injury are usually dead within half an hour, yet somehow, probably because of his immense fitness, Parkin hung on as the helicopter rushed him to hospital. Surgeons cut through his chest to reach his heart. He is now missing some of his left pectoral muscle as a consequence. He'd also broken bones in his left arm – now fused, the elbow bent permanently at ninety degrees – and hip, giving him his characteristic limp. Parkin was a brilliant rock climber before the accident, but he accommodated himself to his new body and he has climbed hard since. 'I always thought there'd be an amazing test one day,' he says of the accident.

I'm not sure Parkin would agree with Nietzsche's suggestion that you should 'make yourself into a piece of art', although that's the modern credo. He'd rather disappear in the mountains than play the publicity game. 'I always saw that as a weakness. That's where you're flawed if you do need that.' The months he spent flat on his back after the accident and the years of slow psychological healing were an ordeal that seems to have tempered his spirit, as a crucible tempers steel. 'I wasn't sure if I wanted it,' Parkin says matter-of-factly. 'You know. Life.' At fifty-four, having made the decision to live, he's turned toward the future. 'Climbing's like a piece of art. Once it's done there's no point waffling on about it afterwards. I'm thinking about the next one now.'

As we climb slowly towards the crag, first through pine trees, then under the full force of the sun, he seems to gather momentum. The steeper it gets, the more natural he looks, first on the approach, and then on the early slabby pitches. I forget his injuries. Maybe he does too. His climbing style is necessarily a little idiosyncratic, requiring little skips to accommodate his hip, and he has to manage his weakened arm. But Parkin retains the natural flow of an instinctive climber. On my first lead, an ibex pokes its head over a ledge just above me. I'm boggled at how it got there.

It seems utterly in its element. Maybe that's my problem. However much I wished it twenty-five years ago, this is not where I belong. For sure, he's come a lot closer to the kind of life he imagined for himself, when he discovered this valley, than I have. Four years after his near-death in Switzerland, he went back to the Himalaya, to Makalu, just to tag along and remind himself of what he used to be. Since then he's travelled the world, climbing new routes and stripping away everything that interrupts his vision. What he does is who he is.

Maybe that's why I'm back home in Sheffield, minding my household gods. Climbing has become a familiar part of my life, like weeding the garden or walking the dog. It's congenial. There's a price for living and creating as Andy does, and it's one I can't afford. Parkin, I realise later, has let me have the crux, for which I'm grateful. It's fun, easy but not too easy, even refreshing. For a moment I let my mind's eye swoop into space to watch me from behind, pinned to the cliff. The tension that's been dragging at my heels since I arrived in Chamonix thaws a little. I laugh to myself. At myself. Just keep going: that's all. We coil the ropes and slip back down to the car.

Back at his studio, drinking tea, he shows me the bicep of his left arm, withered from lack of use.[2] Anatomical reconstruction, coupled with a fondness for *objets trouvés*, is the hallmark of Parkin's sculpture. His studio is littered with bits of wire, metal and glass. 'There's nothing to begin with, you've got to create an object to fill a space,' he explains. 'I start with basic shapes, get some anatomy going, but I want to do it with the minimum. There's a leg or a calf, a nice movement or tension, that's how I want the rest of it to go on. It's the flow of following shapes I find, the way things are dictated to me. There's an element of chance there, which I like, because it keeps the game interesting. I'm trying to be sparing with everything. I don't need much, right? I like the idea of things doing one thing, but also doing something else. Climbing's taught me a lot of that.'

2.   Author's note: In December 2016, Parkin's studio was totally destroyed in a fire.

The sheer mass of stuff he's collected over the years now smothering his studio's workbench is bewildering, although I believe him when he says he knows where everything is. I mention Francis Bacon's notoriously scruffy studio and he laughs. 'You couldn't get through the door of 'is place.' Despite twenty years spent perfecting his French, he's kept his Sheffield accent. He says in another life he could have been an archaeologist. Parkin has produced sculptures in the past from the wreckage of crashed aircraft spat out by the Bossons Glacier. I ask him whether finding things in the mountains has a particular resonance for him.

'It could be a crystal, or a piece of metal. Or part of an ice axe or a karabiner from another age. Something with a story. How did it get there? And you can see the forces of the glacier in it, how they've gone to work on it. It's massively interesting. I'm trying to recycle things, transform them into something else with my own story added on.'

He picks up a sculpture he's been working on. It is spare; the wind could blow through it. 'The brass comes off refuges built on Mont Blanc in the nineteenth century,' he says. 'All that effort and history. Man carried it up there, assembled a little hut to survive in, only for it to get destroyed, swallowed by the glacier, compressed by the glacier, rejected by the glacier and along I come to climb and scoop all these things up. I'm still respecting the efforts of those first men. To me it lends strength. I like to feel part of a continuing line of things, whether as a climber or an artist.'

He turns the copper and glass figure over in his hands. 'There's a lot of superfluous rubbish in climbing. You can always cut it down. Learn to do a lot with a little. There's no point carrying extra weight. Make sure you know what to do with it all. Take pride in it. Maintain it. Tweak it.' That attention to detail, he says, shows the fine art in anything. 'It's the warrior sharpening the sword. Everything's got to be right. You're building yourself up. If you can, spend time fiddling with your kit, looking for details, making things better or more personalised. Make it interesting. Make it yours. That's the point.'

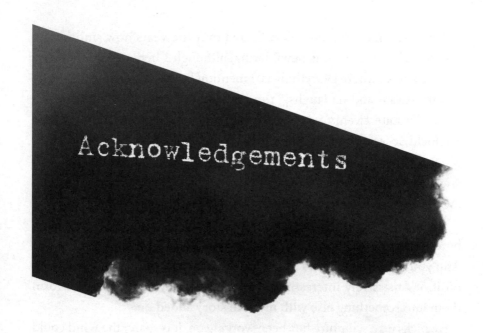

Acknowledgements

I can't remember when I started working for American outdoor magazines, but a few years ago, not altogether consciously, I began to do a lot more of it, most probably because I adore and prefer long-form journalism and that was something increasingly difficult to do in Britain for specialist audiences. I wanted to preserve something of this period in my life, and felt that the eight essays included here were of more lasting value as a snapshot of my own particular interest in climbing and of a few key moments in the activity's long and fascinating history. I am as always indebted to those prepared to talk about their lives and experiences.

I am deeply indebted to the editors I've worked with in the last few years, including Jeff Jackson, Alison Osius and Duane Raleigh at *Rock and Ice*. Having published climbing magazines myself, I know how hard it is, especially now, and I want to acknowledge how much I value their judgement and support. I'd also like to thank Katie Ives at *Alpinist*, whose devotion to the written word and insights as an editor are deeply valued by those who work with her. Writing in the year Ken Wilson died, who was another great mentor, sometimes against my will, I'm conscious how important good editors are to the climbing world, and how rare they are. I also want to thank my friends Jon Barton and John Coefield at Vertebrate Publishing for taking on this quixotic project and seeing it through. The essays have been re-edited, mostly for a British readership.

'The Magician's Glass' appeared in *Alpinist* in Summer 2012. 'Stealing Toni Egger' appeared in *Rock and Ice* in August 2015. 'Searching for Tomaž Humar' appeared in *Rock and Ice* in June 2010. 'Big Guts' appeared under the title 'Free Wheel' in *Rock and Ice* in June 2011. 'Crazy Wisdom' appeared in *Alpinist* in Spring 2015. 'What's Eating Ueli Steck?' appeared under the title 'The Burden of Annapurna' in *Rock and Ice* in October 2014. 'Lone Wolf' appeared in *Rock and Ice* in July 2014. 'Lines of Beauty' appeared under the title 'A Muscular Imagination: Andy Parkin and the Art of Climbing' in *Alpinist* in Autumn 2009.